I0436681

# Why People Still Don't Do Their Jobs

## Why Your Car Was Recalled and Other Interesting Stories

JAMES A. SHELL

© 2024 James A. Shell, All rights reserved.

Copyright Disclaimer under section 107 of the Copyright Act 1976, **allowance is made for "fair use" for purposes such as criticism, comment, news reporting, teaching, scholarship, education and research**. Fair use is a use permitted by copyright statute that might otherwise be infringing.

Other Disclaimer: The content of this book is for entertainment purposes only. It is given in good faith based on my experience as an auditor and quality systems professional. You, the user, are accepting the risk of errors and omissions, bad decisions and implementation issues. Keep in mind that in ISO auditing the auditor is the source of highest variability, and just because I make a recommendation, it doesn't mean your auditor will accept the results. By all means, consult additional resources before relying on any of this advice.

Hiring me as a consultant to help you do these activities is not for entertainment purposes and I do accept reasonable responsibility for errors and omissions.

# Contents

# 01 Introduction

This is the second part of my work on the important topic, "Why People Don't Do Their Jobs."

It's less of a sequel than it is a way to fill in some of the blanks, and highlight higher level, more expensive disasters.

I am qualified to do this because of what I do as a job. I've been auditing the quality systems of "world-class" businesses for a long time, and prior to that have been involved in product development and various aspects of process improvements in an industry that no one used to care about, but at some point, soon, people will care about again.

I have some stories to tell about some of these places.

My job is to go in and make a determination of how their quality systems are functioning. I do about 50 of these audits a year, in all sorts of environments. I've been to whiskey distillers, the dynamite factory, and several places that make bubble wrap. I've been to the place where a crew of workers personalizes the information on your credit card (that magnetic stripe) along with the chip. I've seen concrete outhouses and railroad locomotives fly through the air on giant cranes.

I do a lot of work with people who are recruiters for what are now called "civilian contractors" who are the people that keep the US Military's systems safe from cyberattack, and also, replace their military laptop when someone drives over it with a hummer.

One frequent type of audit is a startup situation. People that want to live out the American Dream by inventing some sort of gadget or service that over a period of time gains market acceptance.

I also audit a lot of family businesses. They have a certain character of their own, and later on, you'll get my nuanced point of view on this type of business.

## Business Improvements

As part of this International Standard, there is a requirement to document something called a "corrective action." That's where there is some kind of screw-up, and some responsible party is required to do an investigation. It is similar enough to the investigation that happens when a plane crashes.

Over the course of my work with these, I've determined that they fall into patterns. I am not the first one who has noticed this.

As part of the investigation, the client is required to do some soul searching, or analyze the cause of the failure. A very typical method for this is called the "Five Why" analysis, which originated with the founder of Toyota in the 1930's. It basically says, in five-year-old fashion that when you have a problem, continue to ask "why" until you get to something that is actionable. I have a clip of this below:

There are "rules" for these things, and ultimately the "rule" is that you can stop asking "why" at the point where you can take some kind of action.

I have to sort of chuckle at this one, which was posted by Indeed:

> ***Problem:*** *Reduced plant output*
>
> 1. *Why? One machine was not functioning properly.*
> 2. *Why? A belt was out of place.*
> 3. *Why? The machine did not receive its scheduled routine maintenance this month.*
> 4. *Why? No service provider was scheduled to perform the maintenance.*
> 5. *Why? The company is negotiating a contract with a new service provider.*
>
> *The manager realizes that no plan is in place for machine maintenance while the company negotiates the new contract. They can now develop a plan to make sure routine maintenance and repairs still occur during the negotiation period.*

In this situation, the plant output was reduced because of "equipment failure" which was due to a belt adjustment not being done.

This was attributed to the company negotiating some kind of outsourced maintenance program, and never addressing the issue,. Can you see the problem with this? The "manager," that is to say whoever is in charge of maintenance, didn't do his job. It's his job to remember and do the maintenance, or tell a subordinate to do so, and prioritize that activity versus negotiate some contract.

Now you get it. This book is being written to get you to the point that you realize someone didn't do his job.

## Improvement Fail

Why did the maintenance guy not do his job? Well we need some more investigation, of course.

Maybe he didn't know that's what his job was. Maybe he knew and blew it off.

He may be "memory impaired." He may be one of the 75% of the workforce that is either disengaged or actively disengaged. He could be overworked and sleep deprived. He could be one of the 10% of the workforce that shows up drunk every day.

In any case, there could be a CMMS system to list all of the daily, weekly and monthly maintenance activity. If that's the case, and it didn't get done, why did that happen?

## Improvement Fail

So that's it. 90% of the 2500 of these I have seen don't ask the "next question." Why did that person not do his or her job?

It might be something perfectly innocent. He may be under pressure to keep the equipment running until the annual plant "maintenance shutdown." There may be a spare parts issue. It could be a number of reasons.

Or, he could be the boss's nephew and just didn't feel like it.

## Who Should Read this Book

The main reader of this book comes from something I will call a little later the "technocratic layer", which is the layer in any social organization that might have the misfortune of being in charge of any of it. It's that layer that has the only chance to fix it.

Chances are the wait person or other low wage worker won't be reading it, unless they're studying management or something, so it's not for everybody.

## The Process Approach

The Quality Systems and Lean Manufacturing people are big into the "process approach."

In this methodology, an operation is broken down into "processes." We're going to do something similar in the next chapter.

Each process has a set of process inputs and process outputs, and any improvements and/or investigations examine the individual parts of this.

There is a process for doing your job, and there is also a process for not doing your job.

Here is a little video to this effect:

https://youtu.be/BbUUSFfQT5c

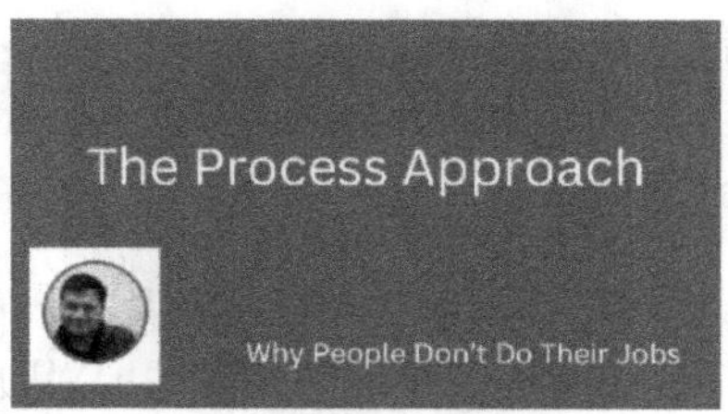


## The Process of Not Doing Your Job

Here it is. You're a mediocre employee who doesn't know what his or her job is, because the job is not well defined and you're poorly trained. You try to do some work but struggle because the equipment is junky, and not made for the amount of throughput that is expected. You're also not completely sure you did your job correctly, since you've never been told the difference between "good" and "not good" and no one knowledgeable is around.

The alarm system, whatever it is, is not able to feed back to anybody that there is a problem, if there is one.

The news of this gets back to your supervisor, who is not all that super, because instead of being hired based on competence and character, he is the boss's nephew.

Instead of helping you solve the problem, if there is one, he or she shrugs it off, and goes back to reading "How to Win Friends and Influence People."

Instead of changing something, you keep running the way you do because it worked perfectly yesterday. "They" appear on the scene. "They" may be a process engineer or other technocrat. Do "they" contribute anything useful? Unlikely.

The whole thing is "managed" by top management, who is in an information bubble, and thinks they're running a world class operation where everybody is above average.

So, the job doesn't get done. The world is a little worse off.

## Further Reading

I tried hard to back some of this stuff up with links and references. There are QR codes and/or links at various points throughout the text.

You should be able to get further background information and maybe learn how to think like a quality systems person. You can take from this a grain of salt because the talking heads, including me, approach a problem with a certain set of biases.

Anything I don't back up is my professional opinion.

All I can do is list my qualifications and experience, which I do at the end, and let you decide whether it is me, or some Gen Z with a website that makes more sense. I also have a website, by the way. It's www.jimshell.com, and I hope you visit often.

If you make it all the way back to "about the author" you will find that I, too, am part of the technocratic layer, for what that is worth. I am not attributing any of this to any conspiracy or anyone being "evil" per se, because I don't think anyone is that well organized. I am attributing a lot of it to something that is called "entropy" which is the fundamental tendency for things to break down to its lowest form of energy.

Links and References

# 02 The Fishbone of Failure and the Wheel of Misfortune

I have to introduce a couple of quality systems concepts. The main one I am calling the Fishbone of Failure, and I also have added one of my own, which is the Wheel of Misfortune.

I have a link in the links and references about the fishbone diagram.

I have been to several conventions of people who make a living in "Quality Systems." These people on the whole tend not to be free-spirited, but it's not as bad as the tax accountants. I am trying to make this understandable and entertaining enough, with enough pictures, to give you a framework to think about some of these issues without your eyes glazing over.

Be patient.

## Fishbone Diagrams

The Lean Manufacturing People love these, as do the quality people. They define a "process" and they split the "process inputs" down into components, which they arrange in sort of a fishbone pattern.

This is another one of those things that has been going on for a long time. It is not my favorite method, but is fairly useful. It was invented by Ishikawa in the 1960's and has become entrenched.

Here is a simple version:

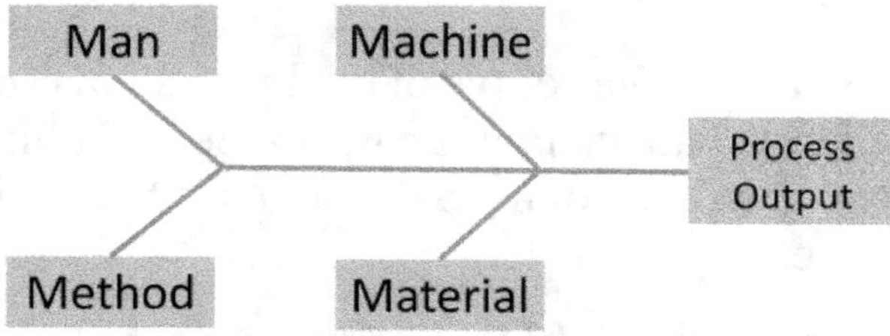


Sorry about the lack of political correctness in the above diagram, the 4 M method of this is an artifact of the culture and time that invented it.

## Process Investigations

This methodology is used to break a process, usually in manufacturing, down to components. Specifically, the process inputs are categorized as man, machine, method and material. There are a couple of others that are thrown in sometimes, such as "mother nature."

These subcategories are each examined for possible reason for the failure.

I've linked a form from the National Traffic Safety Board (NTSB) which is the form that the investigators use when there is an aircraft crash. This form is basically split up in that same way. The pilot, aircraft (including maintenance), airport facilities and weather conditions are all documented. That way, they recognize that there might have been more than one cause, and they at least ask the right questions.

I've also included a couple of links to a couple of fatal hot air balloon crashes, where the number one cause was "operator was loaded."

This is a topic for a future book, I think. Hot air balloons crash with some regularity, and operators are frequently loaded. They must be free spirits, in their way.

## The Fishbone of Failure

Here it is. I've regrouped these slightly because I can, but you get the picture:

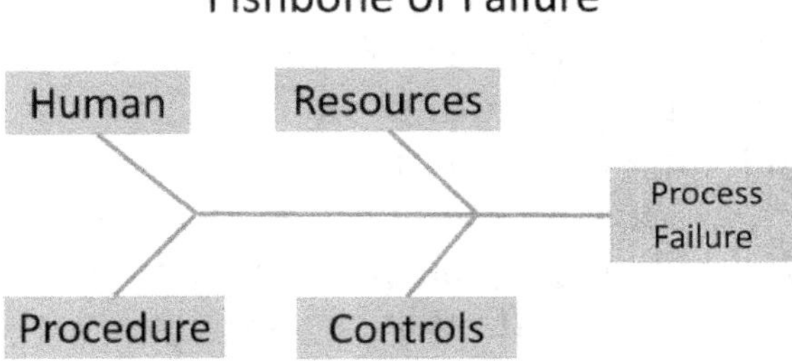


I've grouped process failures into four different categories. It very often happens that there is more than one cause, or contributing factor, to a given process failure.

It also very often happens, as I am about to show you, that the causes all lead back to the same thing.

## The Fishbone of Failure: Human Element

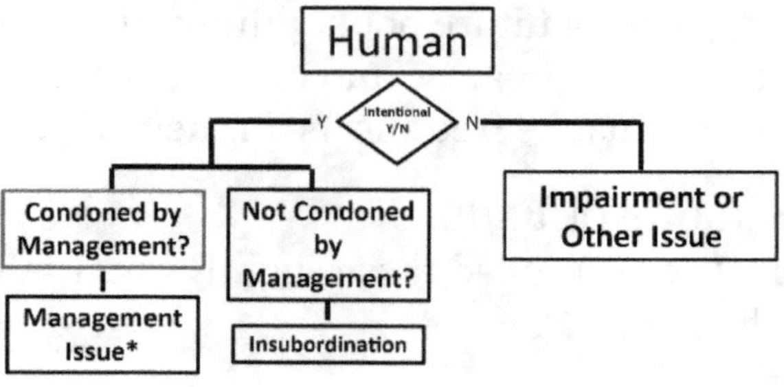


Each of these categories starts out with a working theory, which is that the failure happened in that part of the diagram. I am aware that presupposes a bias toward "blame" and a negative assumption, and as a younger person I might look at this differently, but here is a case where we can have a friendly debate if you wish.

The first question is whether or not the act was intentional or unintentional. There may be some gray area in between. That's up to the investigators to figure out.

Following the "intentional" path, there is a further decision beyond that, which is whether or not the action was condoned by management, in this case this might be a supervisor or other authority figure. If an employee is not doing their job, the management knows about it and condones it, then the problem is with management.

If the employee is intentionally not doing their job, which happens, it could be for a variety of reasons, including sabotage, insubordination, narcissism, having fun, or simply showing off. Or, it could be that the employee feels that the job procedure, or work instruction is screwed up, and made the decision to change without telling anybody. This happens a lot in a place where there are a lot of creative immigrants who have a culture of "making do" and not a culture of "telling the boss."

Different workplaces have different tolerances for this.

## Unintentional Failure

This category is less interesting in a way. It basically says that an employee didn't do his or her job because they can't.

The reason an employee "can't" do their job is widely variable, and at the moment, I am going to refer you to the multiple chapters in the previous book which describe some of these specifically.

Most of the failures on this side of the graph are "actionable," and in these cases, it is possible that they can be the final "why" in one of these root cause analysis 5-Why problems. In this case, there are only two "whys".

| Why | Problem Statement: Hot air balloon crashed into power lines |
|---|---|
| 1. | Pilot forgot power lines were there |
| 2. | Pilot was loaded and decided to fly anyway |

Evidently, the drug testing regimen for hot air balloon pilots is not as stringent as it is for airline pilots for some reason. Who knew?

## Procedure Failure

In most jobs, at the lower levels of the organization there are operating instructions or work instructions or "standard operating procedures." These procedures are not always in writing, but can be. They tell a worker what to do, and how to tell whether or not they've done it correctly. Very often there is a photo or other visual aid about what the finished job looks like.

Have you ever wondered how, when you order something at one of these chain "casual dining" restaurants the dish always looks the same, and always looks like the one in the menu? Well, that's how. There's a photo somewhere in the kitchen that tells the cook what the finished product should look like.

Here's a breakdown:

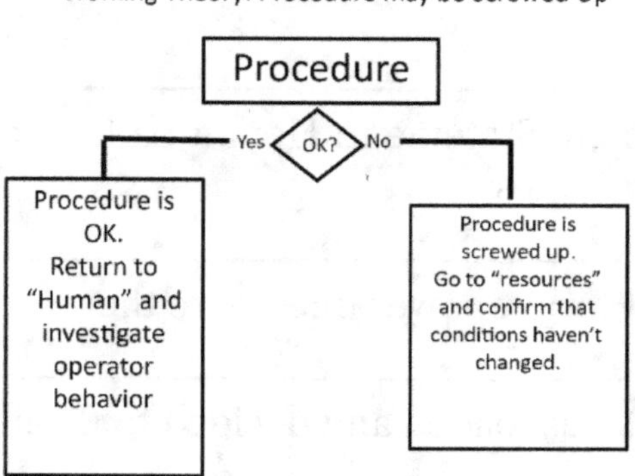
Working Theory: Procedure may be Screwed Up
Procedure
Yes
OK?
No
Procedure is OK. Return to "Human" and investigate operator behavior
Procedure is screwed up. Go to "resources" and confirm that conditions haven't changed.

This was my main job for a long time, by the way. If there was some screw-up in the factory, it was my job to go out and investigate. I would either "certify" that the procedure was being done properly, as a first guess. If not, then most often it was a case where the responsible employee wasn't doing his or her job, at which point I allowed the employee's supervisor to deal with the question of whether it was intentional or not.

In the second case, where, if followed, the screwed-up condition repeated itself, the problem was apparently that there was an issue with the procedure. My mission then became to communicate that back to the people that designed the procedure, or in some cases, I myself was able to make limited adjustments to get the process to work better.

A lot of places have change control systems to keep this from happening without approval from some kind of authority figure.

A lot of jobs have monitoring systems to capture whether or not the employee did his or her job and followed the procedure. An airliner for example has a flight recorder that measures whether the pilot was doing his or her job, and doesn't lie. The proverbial "black box" can be fished out of whatever body of water to get the detailed story of whether the pilot was following his or her procedure.

Either way, it's easy enough to trace this back further to a human, and run the analysis with the next human up the chain of command until you arrive at the source of the problem.

## Resource Failure

By "resource" I mainly mean "equipment" for the moment, but there are lots of other kinds of resources, such as raw materials, servers, IT infrastructure and software, and the like.

My previous book, "Why People Don't Do their Jobs" has a lot to say about this. Ultimately at the end, a significant percent of equipment failure can be traced back to the efforts, or lack of, of a human. A human did the work of designing, selling, buying, installation and operation and maintenance of that equipment. Poorly, in some cases.

Working Theory: Resources may be insufficient or screwed up

Resources

| Reason | Description | Comments |
|---|---|---|
| 1 | Not Reading the Operator's Manual | Ref: "Top Gun Pilots" chapter |
| 2 | Improper Maintenance | The engineers who design and have experience with these things often put information in the operating manual, which is often second-guessed |
| 3 | Poor Electrical Connections ref: dirt and contamination | Dirty connectors is a primary reason for this, which means that someone didn't do the job of cleaning it.. |
| 4 | Overrunning Machine Capacity | See above, this is an artifact of the Dividend Growth Model which says to milk every possible unit out of the equipment you can. |
| 5 | Not replacing worn parts | This is an organizational culture issue. |
| 6 | Misaligned tighteners | This is typical of farm equipment mainly, but there are tighteners on every car and fork lift |
| 7 | Improper storage/shut down | Depending on the equipment shutdown protocol is a key to equipment life, especially in equipment which has a heat/cool cycle. |
| 8 | Weather-related issues | A lot of the responsible farmers of this age have metal buildings or other structures to keep their $250,000 combine from being snowed on. |
| 9 | Ignoring Warning Signals | Ref: Alarm Systems |
| 10 | Untrained Operators | Ref: Temps and Doubtsourcing |

## Workplace Environment

Workplace environment, in my opinion, falls into the category of a resource, in that the management installs, maintains, and condones anything that happens in terms of a work space.

That also extends to the emotional and cultural work environment.

It is a slightly different problem, whether a work environment is physically toxic compared to emotionally, but it is fairly obvious that in either case, it is a management activity to monitor, provide and maintain an environment that is conducive to people doing their jobs.

## Control Systems

There are a lot of different kinds of control systems, and management spends most of their time enmeshed in them.

These include regular alarms, like flashing lights, and complex alarms like stockholder reports and financial statements that give feedback.

If something goes wrong in a business, it almost always happens that ignoring some control system was a contributing factor. I will have much more to say about them later.

Here is a table of control system signals and potential actions.

Working Theory: Control Systems Have Failed

Controls

| Condition (not all inclusive) | Action |
|---|---|
| Alarm System Failure | Go to "resources" and find out why. (eventually leads to Human) |
| Inspector goes to sleep | Go to Human |
| Passes inspection, customers still complain | Go to "procedures" and re-think process for setting quality inspection |
| Fails inspection, management says to ship anyway | Human |
| Fails inspection, stuck with a lot of defective material | Investigate procedures and equipment |

The most frustrating failure mode in this is that the control system signals a failure of some kind, and then "personnel" ignore or overrule it.

The same can be said for most types of controls, or alarms or feedback. If a hundred thousand customers send your crappy item back, it is better to believe them.

## The Wheel of Misfortune

You may remember the "Experience Curve". This says that in the initial stages of a project, the costs are high and throughput is low. As the organization gains experience, production costs decrease.

Well, one of the production costs, supposedly, is the proverbial "screw-up." The more mature the project is, the lower the level of chaos (if the management has done its job).

Figure 1. Forty-percent experience curve

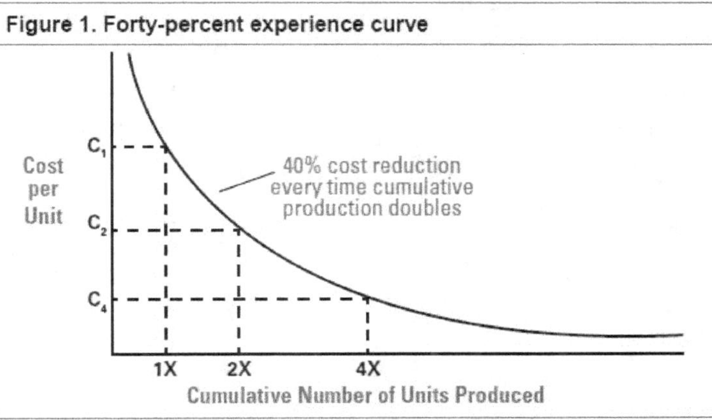


I sourced this from Don Holstrand from Iowa State, and it may be related more to agriculture, but the same concept applies to manufacturing.

The "Wheel of Misfortune" assumes a three-level organization. "Employees" are the hands on operational level. "Supervision" is the authority that trains and monitors them, and "management" is the level that oversees the process and makes decisions.

The "Wheel of Misfortune" measures the probability that a given production issue originated in that layer. "Blame" is a bit harsh.

Until the employees develop dexterity or gain experience in the process, failures are going to be numerous, and small, and appear in the employee layer of the organization. Naturally failures can be reduced significantly by having the process fully developed, and training given before the new process is rolled out.

Of course, it depends heavily on the process. If it is a process that requires manual dexterity, such as assembly or sewing, for example, the absolute number of defects may be higher. If it is an automated process, where the employees just feed the machine, maybe less so.

This also works the same for mature products, where there is a lot of employee turnover and new employees. If enough people quit, it's the same as a startup situation.

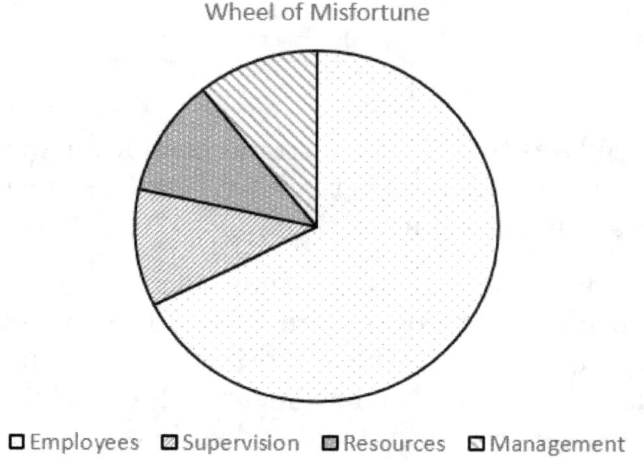


Of course, there is some ownership of this to go around. There may also be equipment tweaks and other adjustments that need to be made.

Once everyone gets trained, some time goes on, and there is some redistribution of this as follows:

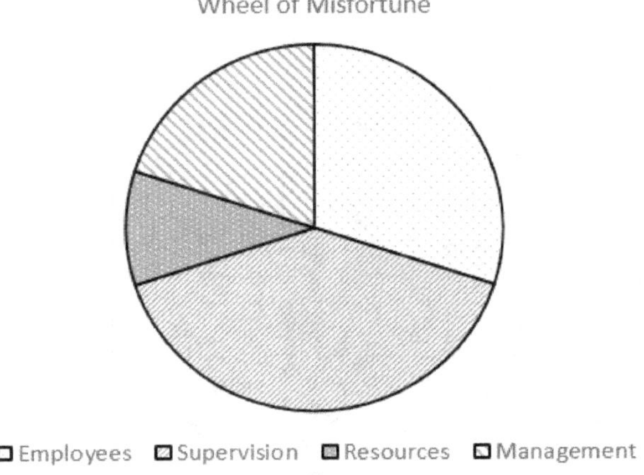


I am ready to say that this roughly represents the C2 phase in the experience graph. There is an overall reduction in the amount of scrap as the employees get more acquainted to the product. In this case the supervisor level begins to own the problems. They're responsible for maintaining controlled conditions.

## Failure Culture

This advanced case, C3 in the graph below, is what we call a culture of failure, and the responsibility for failure falls on management.

The employees should have been trained, and the "supervisory class" including the technical class, should be able to monitor the process and make corrections as needed. The absolute number of failures should be low, because the organization is down the experience curve, but it is not always low.

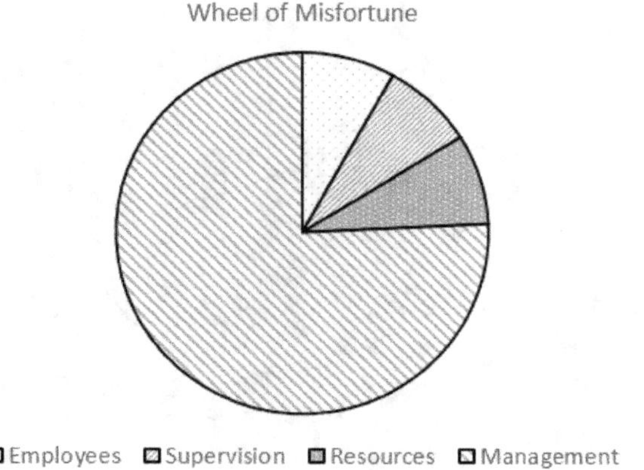


Sometimes it really is still the employees' fault. But at some point, the supervision and management, and eventually just the management, have to own it. My guess is that the Toyota philosophy of not "blaming" the workers started in a mature process.

This is the case where employee disengagement happens. Employee selection becomes terrible, turnover is high, there is constant training, and this comes at a cost.

## The Fishbone of Failure

The Fishbone of Failure is sort of a road map. It is a graphic representation of where in the organization one is likely to find a screw up, provided one wants to know.

Anybody with the misfortune of being in charge of improving quality, or production, could use this. It is a common tool of the "lean" manufacturing people and others.

The Fishbone of Failure is static, and represents a moment in time.

The idea of the Wheel of Misfortune is that it is fluid, and represents a probability. The more mature the product, and the company, the more likely the "problem" originates in supervision and management, with resultant peril for anyone who is trying to fix it.

Keep these things in mind going forward as we explore why people don't do their jobs.

Links and References

Why People Still Don't Do Their Jobs

https://youtu.be/zeJKLOBbYms

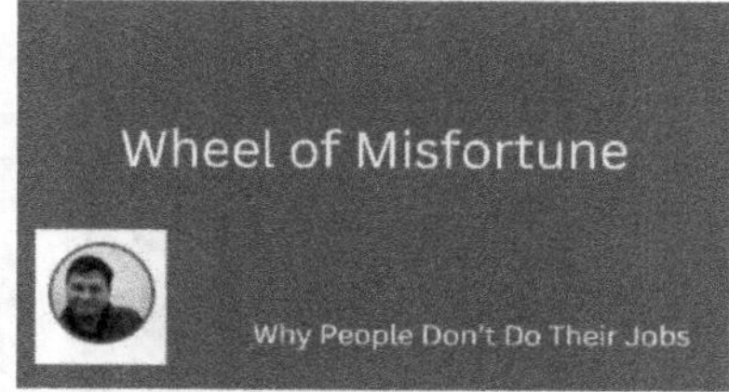

# 03 What to Do if your Boss is an Idiot

In our ongoing study of "why people still don't do their jobs" we're going to spend some time on what to do if the boss is an idiot. I know that seems a bit harsh because bosses are people too, but as we're about to see the problem is widespread enough that a very popular TV show was launched to make fun of it. We all know that having a TV show launched is the ultimate measure of whether something is worth studying.

To be specific, we're going to look at the process of how these people were selected in the first place. We'll spend some time later talking about various examples of idiotic boss behavior.

## Disclaimer

The companies I work for are obvious exceptions to this. This goes double for the companies whose bosses are brilliant enough to hire me as a consultant.

In these enlightened organizations, things run brilliantly, there are never any office problems, and the bosses are all wonderful.

I'm writing this about other companies' bosses, right?

## Search Engine Results

As a public service, I've conducted a survey in the most convenient and cheapest way possible, namely by search engine results.

This is the 21st Century's most accurate way of defining anything. You put something into your favorite search engine, and see how many people searched for it.

| Search | Results |
|---|---|
| What to do if your boss is an idiot | 1,750,000,000 |
| What to do if your boss is incompetent | 7,830,000 |
| What to do if your boss is a compulsive liar | 76,700,000 |
| What to do if your boss is stupid | 99,500,000 |
| What to do if your boss hits on you | 296,000,000 |
| What to do if your boss is mean | 783,000,000 |
| What to do if your boss doesn't support you | 644,000,000 |
| What to do if your boss is slimy | 41,900,000 |

| | |
|---|---|
| What to do if your boss is a terrible leader | 163,000,000 |
| What to do if your boss is spineless | 24,700,000 |
| What to do if your boss is doing something illegal | 143,000,000 |
| What to do if your boss is an asshole | 1,820,000,000 |
| What to do if your boss has bad hygiene | 87,500,000 |

| Search | Result |
|---|---|
| My boss is brilliant | 593,000,000 |
| My boss is highly competent | 93,100,000 |
| My boss is honest | 88,400,000 |
| My boss is intelligent | 554,000,000 |
| My boss has no interest in a relationship with me | 146,000,000 |

| My boss is kind | 835,000,000 |
|---|---|
| My boss is a good leader | 270,000,000 |
| My boss supports me | 1,060,000,00 |
| My boss is brave | 94,000,000 |
| My boss is ethical | 181,000,000 |
| My boss has good character | 1,720,000,000 |
| My boss has characteristics I want | 601,000,000 |
| I am in love with my boss | 807,000,000 |

Someone who is data driven, like me, would hesitate to put an exact number on leader effectiveness in the current era. But, suffice it to say that if three times more people are looking for a solution to an idiot boss than thinks their boss is intelligent, there is a substantial percentage of idiot bosses.

Side point: you know what's fun? The last one. A little novel could be written on the poor person who is in love with their boss, despite idiocy and bad hygiene. Attraction is not a choice.

Why People Still Don't Do Their Jobs

https://youtu.be/SnaEjyfzK-s

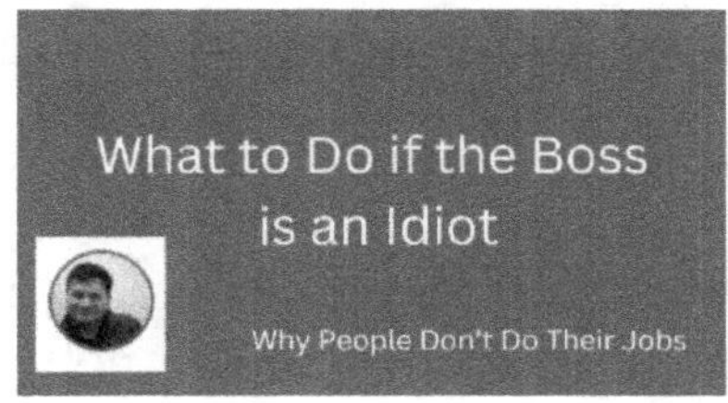

What to Do if the Boss
is an Idiot
Why People Don't Do Their Jobs


## Why is This Important?

This should be fairly obvious but let's boil it down to this: A bad boss impacts mental health, productivity, job satisfaction, and is a major reason for people quitting their job and moving on. It's also a major contributor to workplace screw-ups. Somewhere between 15% and 50% of work in some instances are a waste of time due to a bad boss. 24% of the workforce is working for the worst boss they ever had. 82% of the workforce would quit due to a bad boss.

## How Widespread is the Problem of Bad Bosses?

Well, objectively, this depends entirely on the definition of "bad."

Someone can be a tyrant, and from the employee's point of view be a bad boss, but from the organization's point of view can be brilliant because they meet their short term objectives. The opposite is true. Someone can be a wonderful person, and have baby deer and little birds following them around the office, but not get their workforce to be productive. So, this is inherently a balancing act.

In fact, I have a story on this. I worked at a place that had a night shift, and the night shift consisted of mostly immigrants. There was a language barrier and so they made the most English-speaking one of them the Supervisor, so as to communicate with Management.

A few years went by, and the night shift performed adequately. It was productive, there were never any real problems and the situation was controlled. In the eyes of the management this fellow was competent.

But it later came to light that he was charging his employees $10 a night for the privilege of him not firing them. That's better known as extortion. This went on long enough for this fellow to afford a nice truck.

At one point, there was a union election, and the union won. The first meeting was held, and the union representatives said "Let's talk about this night shift supervisor." At that point, with some embarrassment, the fellow was fired. So, from the point of view of the management, this fellow appeared fine, but from the employees' point of view he was terrible and a bad boss.

Anyway, the search engine data above can and should be discounted appropriately. But, to make a long story short, the preponderance of these surveys says that the problem is very widespread

## TV Bosses

We could, and probably should, do a whole book on this topic, and how this has evolved through the years. I am not going to do too much better than the article that I have linked in the links and references, highlighting the best and worst TV bosses, except to say that the definition of a "good boss" has changed throughout the years as well.

Let's start with the cartoon bosses from the early 1960's, Mr. Slate and Mr. Spacely. These were the TV bosses for the Flintstones and Jetsons, respectively. Both of these characters were assumed to be competent, humorless, and demand the respect of Fred and George, the congenial main characters.

I'm going to give you the theory that they represented the "military hierarchy" management approach of that era. A lot of the workforce, and a lot of the society was still being influenced by the work ethic of the 1939-1945 period, which only happened 15 years before. You didn't think too much about your boss's competence, your job was to follow orders. Both Fred and George were a little afraid of their bosses, who fired them occasionally.

Captain Kirk, the Star Trek boss fell roughly into this category as well.

## Cultural Shift

I'm also ready to say that the most famous TV boss of the current era, Michael Scott on "The Office" represents the evolution of the TV boss into helpless buffoonery. The other option on this is the TV boss as "supervillain", namely Mr. Burns from The Simpsons.

I have a couple of references in the links and references that list the most toxic TV bosses. For the moment we will put off the project of defending the "cultural shift" attribute of this, unless you want to engage me in televised debate, which I get the broadcast rights to.

Unless you are Tony Stark, the boss of "The Avengers" superheroes, you are likely in this era to be either evil or a boob.

## How did this happen?

Let's say, hypothetically, you have a simple work group, with a three-tiered organizational structure. Most economic entities in this era are still organized in that way. There may be an extra tier or two or three depending on the immensity of the organization.

You, the "top manager," have an opening for a supervisor, and want to pick from among your employees the best person to fill it. How do you choose?

We will tackle the possibility of bringing in someone from outside to fill the position at some other point. Based on my observation, of several hundred companies over a period of years, I'd have to be convinced that it makes any difference.

## The Character Ethic

I'm going to borrow from Stephen Covey, "Seven Habits of Highly Effective People" for this idea.

He says that prior to 1920, bosses were hired on the basis of the "character ethic." That is to say, if the top management of a business needed a group leader or middle manager, they chose based on character elements. These included integrity, humility, hard work, loyalty, self-control, courage, justice, patience, modesty, and morality. If you promoted someone like that, you weren't sure if he would be an effective boss, but were fairly sure that the person was going to be respected by the workforce.

## The Most Dangerous Book Ever Written in English

It's "How to Win Friends and Influence People" by Dale Carnegie. This book is written based on the "personality ethic", which is to say, a person may focus on short cuts and manipulation to get what they want.

Dale Carnegie Training Video

https://youtu.be/aqF9Wo3NEoc?si=oBIgYWqMf-a-7yoY

Dale Carnegie, by the way, grew up in Northwest Missouri. He started by selling correspondence courses to the local farmers, and then selling lard and bacon for the Armour company. He had accumulated $500 at the age of 23, and moved to New York, to attend the American Academy of Dramatic Arts, with the idea of becoming a Chautauqua lecturer.

He was a pioneer of what we now call "development training" and founded a company for this purpose.

Ultimately, he invented "multiple revenue streams" by selling collections of his writings, and by the time of his death in 1955, had over 450,000 graduates of the "Dale Carnegie Institute." This company is still around 70 years later, and still producing revenue for someone. It fits perfectly into the current model of web-based training, seminars, and you can still get the original book, which was produced in 1936.

## What's wrong with this?

As it applies to management, it basically says that there is a way other than working hard and being knowledgeable to have your boss like and promote you.

We should talk about whether or not "wanting a promotion" is a good thing. In 1936 it was considered desirable, but now, there is a certain fraction of the workforce that doesn't want to be promoted. The primary reason is that 39% of companies will offer you more responsibility but not increase your pay.

But assuming they want higher status in an organization, "getting the boss to like you" is a means for a friendly idiot that follows the formula to get it.

The problem is that eventually, the company is run by people that look good and are friendly around the office, but don't know anything about the processes or products, which is to say, the boss is an idiot.

## The Peter Principle

This was a book by Laurence J. Peter and Raymond Hull. The basic theory is that in any complex organization, in which there is a hierarchy, there is a tendency for most of the positions in higher levels of the organization to be populated by people that are incompetent.

The basis of this is that someone who is technically competent and capable of their job at one level will get promoted. In an organization with multiple levels, this can happen several times. Eventually, they will rise to the point at which they can no longer be promoted i.e. are incompetent.

This book was written in 1969, which is very near the year of "peak everything" and is an artifact of the giant organizations with many levels, which were common at the time.

Since that time, because of the technological revolution and other things that have gone on in the economy, the expectations are a little different. However, the underlying theory, that is to say, people being placed into jobs that they are temperamentally or intellectually unsuited for, is very valid.

## The Dilbert Principle

In 1995 the comic strip writer Scott Adams coined the Dilbert Principle. It states that an organization actually promotes the least competent employee in a work group. The underlying theory is that this employee is being put into a position where they can do the least damage, management, in which case the engineers can get their work done.

The problem with this is that it is contagious, and eventually all of the upper levels of an organization will be filled with the least competent employee possible, which then leads to toxic workplaces and overall organizational dysfunction.

This is also an artifact of the era. This was shortly after the invention of the cubicle, and during the period of software farming and other high-tech activities. In that era, the employees were very often more technically knowledgeable than the management in a given activity.

https://youtu.be/u3yoUprjkNs

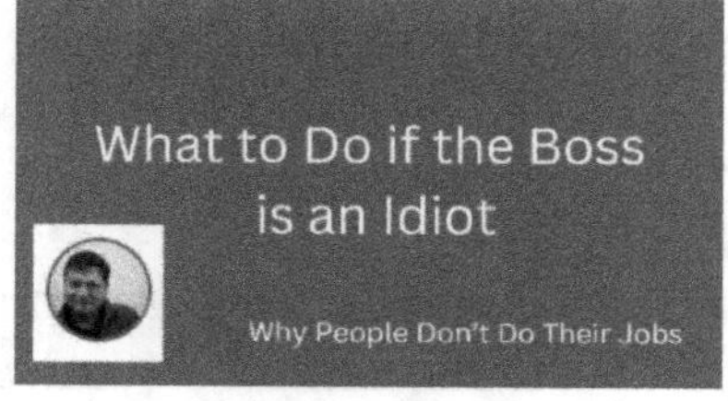

What to Do if the Boss
is an Idiot
Why People Don't Do Their Jobs


## Current Developments

I work with several different companies in which there is no such thing as "office politics". These companies use a lot of remote workers, and have clearly defined tasks and roles, and an army of remote employees working in their spare bedrooms across the land.

These organizations are doing data handling and the one I am thinking of at the moment requires its remote workers to have some technical competence in the industry in which the data is being generated. They have a small office someplace, where a handful of managers try to organize all of the activity.

The "managers" in these places are typically the most experienced and technically competent employees, and the "line employees" who can be subcontractors have no place to hide. Their keystrokes and other activities are monitored electronically. If someone doesn't do their job, or does their job badly, this is objectively measured and dealt with.

In these places, at least at the low levels, the bosses tend not to be idiots. However, the bosses may tend to be slave drivers, and since anyone in these situations are candidates to be replaced by AI at some point, there is some question as to whether one of these jobs is any better. Some people like their bosses to be idiots.

## What To Do If Your Boss Is an Idiot?

A bad boss impacts employee productivity, quality, job satisfaction and people showing up for work. It is a main reason for people not doing their jobs.

Various systems have evolved throughout the industrial revolution to select leaders who will motivate employees and get them to be engaged in their jobs.

Because of human factors, and other factors, some of which we have already discussed, this very often ends up in failure. Part of why it is a failure is because it is hard to measure, and as we have discussed previously, If any other area of the organization had a 50% failure rate, the company would go broke, so another reason for this failure is that it is tolerated.

What does this mean to me, a person who derives a revenue stream out of human failure? Well, I'd have to say we're living in a golden age.

Links and References

# 04 Mediocrevisors

Mediocrevisors are a lot like supervisors, except they're not all that super.

They're the main line of communication between management and employees, in a certain size of organization. They're also information gathering people, and have a variety of other useful functions in the organization.

Or not. It depends on the organization.

Just to be clear, we're about the spirit of the position now, and not the actual name of the job. This job has a lot of different names. NCO, Foreman, Overseer, Superintendent. It all comes to the same.

The role of the supervisor in the life of the employee is often more powerful than that of a family member. When some of these employees get up in the morning, and look in the mirror, they see the supervisor looking over their shoulder.

https://youtu.be/If4GWw_SsXM

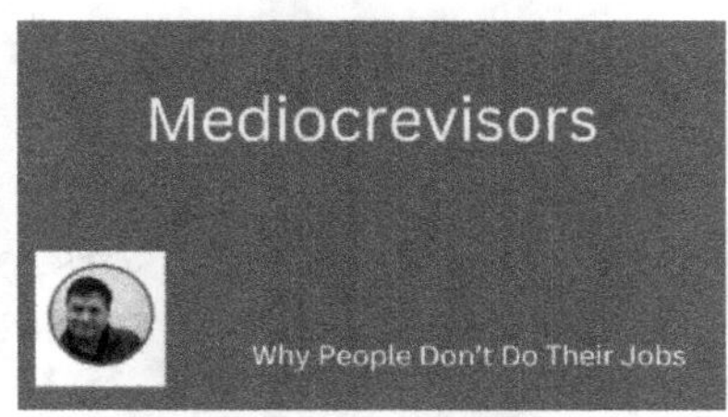


Take that for what it is worth. The supervisor is the face of the organization, in the eyes of the employees.

So, if the supervisor is mediocre, the employees will not do their jobs.

## Ways Supervisors Use to Get People to Do Their Jobs (Historical)

If you want to get Biblical about this we can. Here are some of the ways:

Beating, whipping, chaining them to their work station and starving them, verbally abusing them, punching them, whacking them, and threatening to cut off one or more of their body parts. Intimidating them by threatening their families. Making them fearful by convincing them they will burn in hell if they don't work.

Hanging the slowest three people in front of the plant at the end of the work day.

Bringing them in as indentured servants and then threatening to send them back to their own country if they don't work.

PS: Some of this is going on today, in the "less civilized" parts of the world.

## Ways Supervisors Use to Get People to Do Their Jobs (Current)

Paying them. Persuading them. Motivating them. Setting up the job itself so that it is easy to do. Making sure they have enough equipment, of the right type, to do their jobs.

We can only hope that we don't have to end up like the old system.

## The Fundamental Reality of Work (and Supervision)

We've talked several times about the job of management being to maximize the wealth of the shareholders.

We haven't discussed this basic transaction from the worker's point of view.

In a job where a worker is inserting a square peg into a square hole, assembly line or similar, it is fairly easy to see if they've done that to a sufficient degree. Some people get paid by the piece, which is to say that at the end of the day, you count the number of pieces, and pay them X number of dollars per piece. An Uber driver right now is like that, or maybe some truck drivers. They get paid X number of dollars per mile driven.

So, in that case it's easy. But what about jobs where it is not as clearly defined.

Most of the time people are paid based on the number of hours they show up, which in North America right now, is around 40 a week. As Peter points out, you're paid for input and not necessarily for output.

The new paradigm for remote workers is to pay the workers for the length of time they are at their desks, logged on to "Teams" or whatever the equivalent is. I will have to be convinced that it makes any difference.

In either of these cases, capitalism has yet to figure out a way to compensate people for the amount of output, which is what an employer uses to benefit the business in some fashion. Someone could log in, work slowly, and get paid the same amount as his or her neighbor in the next cube who is all stressed out and overworked.

Or in the Dale Carnegie world of work, someone could show up five minutes before the boss, greet everybody warmly in the office, bring everyone coffee and donuts on Friday, run the office Fantasy Football league, spend a lot of water cooler time, and never actually accomplish anything during the day. But in Dale Carnegie World, these are the people that are going to be promoted in the workplace because they are "team players," whatever that means.

Furthermore, the question of unpaid overtime comes up. In some jobs there is an expectation that the worker stays at his or her desk into the evening sometimes, without consideration of extra compensation.

Employees do it anyway because they want to contribute to the success of the business, and also, they hope that it will be rewarded in the long run by some kind of promotion or extra love.

But what happens if that goes on for a long time and there is no extra love, or promotion or anything else? The Japanese workers, who are legendary for that kind of behavior, are also well known for their burnout and passing away at their desk from overwork. Americans did not have as much tolerance for that stuff anyway, but one of the things you're seeing in the "great resignation" is that you're expendable, and people have much less tolerance for what used to be called "dedication."

In some situations, it becomes true that the worker is going to try to minimize the amount of work they have to do in that time period and still get paid.

So, it's the supervisor's job to try to get employees to do at least the minimum amount of work, or preferably more than the minimum, in exchange for the appropriate amount of reward. This may include pay, or other types of rewards. So that's the whole job of the supervisor. Create the conditions by which a worker can do at least, and preferably more, than the minimum amount of work possible, and set out the expectations for "output" to the extent it can be defined.

That can be done in a variety of ways, but legally and morally, they are limited as to how they are allowed to do this.

## The Supervisor's Actual Job

So now you can see the creative tension. How do you know a supervisor is doing his or her job?

If people don't do their jobs, I am going to go out on a limb and say that some front-line supervisor is involved.

No one is saying that this is easy, by the way. As we're finding out, it's hard to get people to do their jobs, particularly certain people, and particularly the supervisors.

It makes sense for the level of management to hire and train the best people that are able to do that. We had a whole chapter on this, to the effect of how to choose, from within or outside the organization, the best people to do that. One of the problems is that a good worker, namely one who put forth greater than the absolute minimum amount of effort, won't necessarily make a good Supervisor.

## Measurements of a "Good Supervisor."

The best way is to measure the output of the organization that he or she is supervising. In manufacturing, as we saw above, that is fairly easy. You do measurements, and there are expectations, and if the department is "meeting its numbers" then maybe the supervisor is doing his or her job.

But in some industries, and in some activities, it is less easy to measure. "Designing" is one of these. How long does it take a competent "designer" to "design" anything?

It is also true that the supervisors are employees too, and have the same tendency to be ticked off, impaired, under-educated, disengaged and have a lot of the other things going on that a regular employee does.

## The Supervisor Hammer

The supervisor usually has one ultimate option to get people to do their jobs, which is that if they don't, to fire them.

We have already talked about this briefly, but to make a long story short, this is thought of as less desirable for a number of reasons. Normally there are experience effects, which means that an experienced employee is more able to do their job than someone off the street. The other thing is that recruiting, hiring someone and then having to train someone costs time and money, and the organization doesn't really want to do that unnecessarily.

But, to the extent that an employee will work a little harder if they are fearful of getting fired, this is a useful tool to counterbalance some of the other tendencies.

## How Can You Tell the Difference Between a Supervisor and a Mediocrevisor?

So now we're down to this: How can you tell the difference between a supervisor and one that is not all that super. In my experience a big predictor is how they spend their time. Here is some data from the McKinsey Company which is a management consulting company.

This graph is for supervisors in various industries:

We're interested in the "Site Level" managers in the manufacturing industry, because when the manufacturing Renaissance happens, which it will, you're going to have to know this.

In this industry, the typical supervisor spends only about 15-25% of his or her time actually supervising anybody. Half of their time is spent in administration and/or meetings, and the remainder is spent doing something called "other."

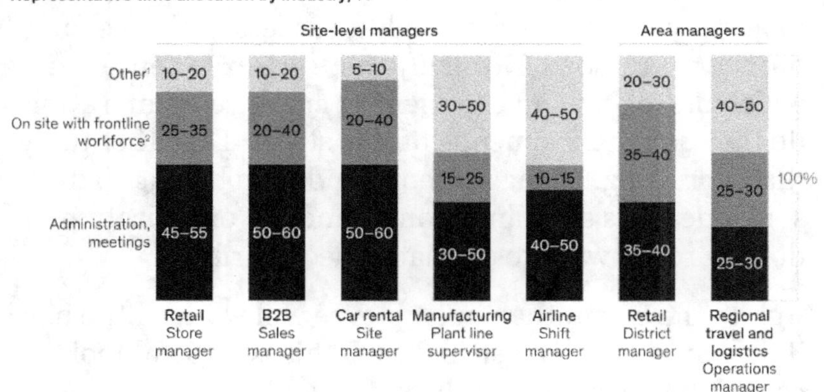


So, what the hell is "other?" I suppose it varies by the supervisor, but I am ready to say a significant fraction of it is sitting in some air-conditioned office filling out the fantasy football worksheet for the week.

## Easier way to Tell

In my role as quality auditor, I have found that all I need to do is go out onto the floor, and stand there. I am required to have an entourage, and that makes me even more conspicuous.

If the supervisors scatter, like those bugs that disappear when you turn the light on, they're not all that super. The correct response by a supervisor to any stranger in their department is to approach them professionally and ask them what they are doing there.

## Alternative Approach: Supervisor Standard Work

There is a lot in the literature from the deep thinkers of this field on something called the "supervisor standard work" or the Leader Standard Work.

This thing lays out a daily and weekly schedule of required activities for a supervisor in an operation, and it highlights the key things that a supervisor actually needs to do, which is to go out and supervise.

Here is an example: The system basically has his or her routine scripted out for them, and this might include daily and weekly duties of one kind or another

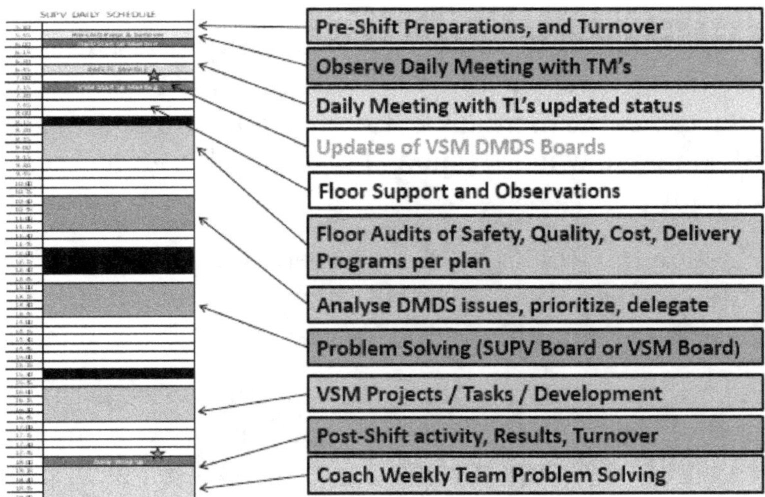


Standard Work for Supervisor

The Supervisor Standard Work or Leadership Standard Work lays out a list of required items for a supervisor to do. In the beginning of the shift, he or she runs the daily meetings, and then hits the floor to do a Gemba Walk or something similar to clear up any issues in the department.

They spend time on the floor doing audits of operating procedures and that kind of thing, and then updating visual aids that are in the department. The idea is that the crew will eventually get on the right side of adulthood and do their jobs.

What this doesn't have in it is a lot of boring meetings. It requires some alignment internally in the organization to keep any meetings short and get the supervisors back onto the floor.

The Supervisor Standard Work is auditable, as well, so that some even higher authority can call the supervisor out if they're not meeting expectations.

## The Number One Problem with Supervisors

They don't see themselves as management. They have not crossed the line mentally between production employee and someone who is responsible for what is going on in the company.

In fact, in the worst cases, the supervisor will build a little fiefdom, where they represent themselves as the authority figure, rather than the actual management of the company.

In some places, being chosen to be a supervisor is the best thing ever. The supervisors get together in some kind of air-conditioned supervisor office, and surf the web or watch some streaming video of some type. If the workforce is experienced and motivated, this works. If the workforce is ticked off, disengaged, impaired, and has personality disorders, it is not so good.

Upper management is very often confused about this. They think "oh, production is running fine, and our new supervisor is doing well." Except, of course, he or she is not doing well.

## Another Alternative to Supervision

A lot of the places that I go to have actually greatly reduced the number of supervisors, and have gone to "lead operators." The "lead operator" is an experienced equipment operator or regular employee that has some additional responsibilities. These include working with scheduling, working with work assignments on the line, and a lot of administrative work that was once done by the supervisors.

There is also a training role. When someone new comes into the organization, the lead operator has some training responsibility.

The typical line seems to be discipline. If there is a need for disciplinary actions, one of the few supervisors is brought in to do it.

The benefit of this system is that it takes away some element of the "fear and intimidation" out of the supervisor/boss relationship. The lead operator is, after all, one of the workers. But the organization has to have a pretty mature workforce in order for this to work, because there is an assumption that the majority of the team members will be cooperative.

In the reference I have linked, there is actually a standard work for a "lead operator" so this concept can be extended to this level in the organization as well.

## Supervision Caveats

There are a couple of other things.

First of all, there is such a field of study as "employment law" and that is to protect the workers from a supervisor being "abusive." There are a lot of labor laws, and discrimination laws, and those kinds of things that need to be followed for protection of the workers.

In this era, as in the past, some workers are fearful. At the very minimum, a supervisor needs to be aware of the limits of his or her job function as it applies to safety, workplace social environment, harassment, and everything else.

I haven't talked about unions very much, but unions developed in the first place because of exactly that kind of thing. During periods of economic trouble, a supervisor can use his or her authority to abuse people and that is not acceptable under any circumstances. The management hammer is that a supervisory role can be used as a weapon, or a means of extortion.

## Cultural Issues

In addition to navigating the law, there are workplace cultural issues.

Right now, because of workplace discrimination and a lot of other issues going on in the society, an organization needs to be careful to be aware of cultural and racial politics.

To put it perfectly bluntly: If the management is a lot of middle-aged white guys, and the workforce is a lot of low wage African American people, you have a potential problem. The chances of the workforce being ticked off is very high, and frankly I don't blame them.

They may go so far as to have workplace violence.

However, if you then make the supervisor in the same work group an African American person, you might get more acceptance from the employees, but there are potential loyalty issues if the supervisor can't get mentally into the role of being a member of management.

The Japanese operations seem to have figured that out. In most of these places, the local "plant manager" who runs the plant on a daily basis is an American, but in the background, there is a "Japanese boss" that actually is running the place.

In a general way, it is a good business practice to have an ethnic or religious labor force that is roughly the same as the local population. That tends to be less of a problem, and the same is the same for the upper-level staffing.

We have not progressed to the point that everybody in the organization is aligned on taking care of the customers, and everyone will be working for the overall good of the organization. That will be left to the robots I am afraid. Humans usually fall short of that as a metaphysical ideal.

## Supervision, 1930-1968.

The activity was Railway Track Maintenance, and the supervisor was this fellow in the middle who was my grandfather.

He was a bit too young for World War 1 and considered essential for World War 2, and was a lover and not a fighter.

His first supervisory job was to manage one of those big railroad crews during the Depression. These crews ranged from 25-100 employees, and performed various operations such as replacing ties, replacing and aligning track, tearing out switches, and other repairs that happen due to normal wear and tear.

If there was a derailment, or washout, or sun kinks, part of the crew were called out to deal with it. In the summer there were "extra gangs" which had a lot of temporary workers. These were typically the scum of the earth that couldn't get a job elsewhere. This was all manual labor in those days. There were no computerized pieces of track equipment, or tampers or liners to pick up the track hydraulically.

From what I understand, the first day he was put in charge of the crew, the Roadmaster, who was the boss of that section of line, handed him a track shovel, and told him to help his crew scoop some rock. His response to that was to throw the shovel into a nearby cornfield, and explain (with profanity) to the boss that he was a supervisor and he was going to supervise.

At some point, he was put in charge of the big track crews. His basic approach to supervision was when everyone was gathered together on the first day, show up about five minutes late. Figure out who on the crew had the biggest mouth and fire him. Pick out the quietest guy, and make him the timekeeper. No one messed with him after that.

## Supervision Qualities

Aside from putting up with no bullshit whatsoever, he had a few important qualities. He was highly competent technically, having worked on every bit of the line at one point or another. He also was unfailingly dedicated.

At one point in the 1960's he was driving one of those high railed pickup trucks on some two-lane road in Nebraska. Ahead of him was one of those old Winnebago motor homes, trying to pass a tractor. As the Winnebago pulled into his lane, he noticed two little kids in the window above the cab, and decided to ditch it rather than do the head on collision.

The accident happened on a Friday night, and he was in surgery on Saturday, and back at his desk on Monday morning, because it would have been considered a lost-time accident. He wanted his division to get the safety award, which they did.

He was so revered by at least some of his crew that when he finally retired, they chipped in and bought him a little boat, which I inherited.

## Supervision Story, 1975

In one of my two summers on the railroad, I was in a crew of about 25 workers, trying to rebuild a switch in the Omaha switchyard.

The supervisor on that job was the son in law of one of the legendary tyrant bosses that were on the line. Surely, he is long gone by this time. Anyway, this fellow tried to emulate the father-in-law with no success, because, frankly, he wasn't very smart, and could not read a simple blueprint.

These switches are not mechanically complicated, but you have to put the ties in properly. There are switch ties, which are more than twice as long as a normal railroad tie. Also, there are smaller versions depending on where along the switch they go. These things were heavy, and it took eight or more people to lift and move one, jam it under the switch, and then spike it in place, and scoop ballast under it. My job was to help lug the tie and scoop the ballast; I was not the most proficient at running the spike maul.

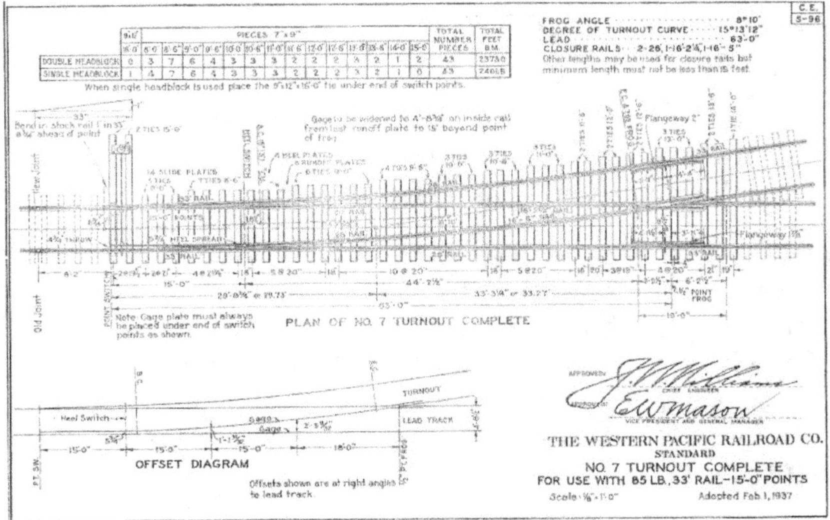


Well, this guy was such an idiot that we ended up rebuilding the switch three times because he couldn't figure out the tie order.

At one point, he docked three guys 10 minutes pay for "bullshitting" that is, standing around chatting while he struggled to find the right ties.

But he managed to screw up the time cards, paying the workers for 0.10 hour instead of 0.90 hours.

The sum total of this was a complete lack of respect of the workforce for this knucklehead, who was projecting his own insecurity onto us, and at the same time, technically incompetent.

## Qualities of a Good Supervisor (in this era)

Well, the references seem to value communication skills, compassion, ability to delegate, being flexible, being a problem solver, being humble, and having a passion for the organization.

It is also not completely obvious but it is the supervisor's job to remove road blocks and also provide resources so that the work group has a chance to do its job.

It remains to be seen whether either of these railroaders from years ago would have lasted long in this era. In fact, the railroads have done away with a lot of this work, and hired outsourcing companies to do the same thing, with even cheaper labor, so a likely career path nowadays might be to start and finish with the outsourcing company, like RJ Corman.

In the previous system, where supervisor was a union position, at least everybody knew that the supervisor had some seniority, i.e. had been around for a while. That didn't necessarily make him good, but at least he knew which end of the shovel to use.

The workforce nowadays for this type of job is also different. Maybe with the machines, the work is less hard than it used to be. That being the case, the supervisor's job is different.

Links and References

# 05 People Don't Know What Their Job Is

A common reason that people don't do their jobs is that they don't know what their job is. This failure mode is fairly logical in that if someone doesn't know for sure what their job is, they can't do it. The prevalence of this is surprisingly high, somewhere between ½ and ⅔ of employees are unclear what their roles and responsibilities are on a given day.

Lack of understanding of job roles and responsibilities leads to inefficiency, duplicated effort, unclear performance measurements, and lack of employee satisfaction. It also has a chance to lead to customer satisfaction and quality issues.

It also makes people crazy and want to quit.

## Job Description History

In most cases, peoples' job responsibilities are communicated via what is normally called a "job description" or "position content document."

This was invented as far back as 1911 by Frederick W. Taylor, the originator of "scientific management", and expanded by the Gilbreths. They proposed something called a "job analysis" that in detail explained exactly what job activities were going on, and identified a set of skills and characteristics of the employee needed for each.

That way, in an assembly line situation, they could clearly organize the work and from that improve efficiency by identifying redundancies and overlap. They could also do training to improve specialization, making the whole operation more efficient.

This was fine, and worked well in one of these manufacturing environments. It works less well in an office and service environment, where the process inputs and outputs are not as tangible.

## The Current State of Job Descriptions

At the current time, based on the reference I have listed in the links, up to 71% of prospective employees feel that job descriptions are vague, 49% of them have annoying buzzwords or internal jargon, and about half feel that job descriptions ask too much of the candidates.

The reason this is important is that at the current time, in the post-Covid environment, a substantial fraction of the workforce has quit, "quiet quit", or is otherwise become disengaged from their jobs.

Suffice it to say at the moment that it's pretty important to attract new employees, and place them in jobs that match their skills and experience. One of the sources says that up to ⅓ of the workforce can be expected to "turn over" in a given year.

If you, as an organization, don't have a way to define peoples' jobs, you have a lot of unqualified people trying to do jobs, and we all know what a mess that is. That's one of the reasons customer experiences are so terrible in this era. People get hired who don't match their actual job requirements, and they can't do their jobs.

## Outsourcing and Contract Work

I have to throw this in as well. Most contract work, particularly in the IT sector, functions based on a "scope of work." This is a detailed description of exactly what the contractor's job is, what the measurements and expectations are, and how the results are communicated.

The "scope of work" enables both parties in the contract to clearly define whether or not the contractor has done his or her job.

"Contractor," could be an individual or organization. It enables something that is very important, which is the billing process. If a contractor does his, her or their job, they can send in the bill and expect to get paid. This is now a substantial portion of the economy is working right now.

I, the little economic entity of one, am very careful when I do this.

So, there's nothing in the water here in the US that causes the rest of the nation's economy to be unable to come up with a clear job description.

## Bad Job Descriptions

There are two main goals of a job description: It clearly defines what a job consists of, so that the candidate knows what their job is supposed to be. It also allows "market communications" to allow the company to attract enough, but not too many, appropriate candidates.

The reference I have linked, which was presented by someone whose job it is to write job descriptions, identifies the following as elements of a bad job description. We'll actually find a couple in a minute.

Because of the search engine thing, and electronic job board thing, which are now the predominant ways that people look for jobs and are hired, the general rules for this have to evolve to follow "search engine rules". The job titles should be searchable, the content of the job should be featured upfront, the salary and benefits should be discussed early on, and from there, the candidate should be able to tell roughly what the qualifications and expectations are.

A bad job description contains some or all of the following elements:

*Long job titles (Hiring candidates who are scanning job boards don't like that).*

*Clever job titles (what on Earth is a "Digital Overlord?")*

*Start with "About Us" (Candidates don't have the attention span and need to know about the job first)*

*Have a lot of legalese (Red flag to some prospective employees)*

*Written in the "Third Person". This sort of depersonalizes the position and turns some applicants off.*

*Show bias (Gender, age, race)*

*Use complex words*

*Fail to talk about benefits or salary*

*Too long or too short*

## Examples

The first one violates about six of the 9 "do not do" things we just talked about. It's for a "Store Protection Specialist."

What's that? Well, after reading it, it looks like this is the person that stands at the door and deters shoplifters. It's the Mall Cop.

You have to work pretty hard to tell what the job is.

Qualifications

- Business Acumen
- Collaborates
- Leading by Example
- Ability to work effectively in a fast-paced environment
- Strong communication skills
- Demonstrated ability to build and maintain relationships with the Store team

7 more items

Responsibilities

- This position provides a visible presence at the Store entrances/exits, mitigating theft and fraud and maintaining a safe and secure environment for Associates and...
- æcommand?g presence in a Company issued vest/required black attire, and monitoring the Code 50 package inspection policy
- Walks sales floor to identify and address potential theft indicators, as directed by Store Leadership
- Partners with Store Leadership to ensure compliance with Loss Prevention directives and minimization of operational shortage
- Must embrace Company values and have a mentality to protect the Ross treasure

Here are some other problems. The requirements and duties are much too long to fit on one page. There is also nothing on here in the "easy to read" part that is objective. You have to scroll down about four pages before you find out that you need to pass a background check, and have a high school education, and that you'll be expected to be on your feet for 8 hours. They also want you to have a security guard license, whatever that is.

Does your typical high school graduate in this era know what "acumen" is? I will let you be the judge. Is it likely that this person will, at some point, not do their job? I'd have to say it's inevitable.

Here's another one. It's the "Executive Assistant" for the local NBA team.

Responsibilities:
• Manages executive administrative level tasks to aid in the success of the EVP & Chief Revenue Officer and any direct reports; manages and processes confidential and sensitive correspondence; manages complex calendar to determine strategic use of EVP's time.
• Interacts with a wide variety of internal and external audiences, including high-level leadership, ownership, staff and external service providers while scheduling appointments, meetings and travel; coordinates itineraries and travel arrangements; serves as communications liaison with internal and external partners and develops materials for communications uses (both electronic and traditional); prepares and submits financial paperwork such as reimbursements and expense requests to the fiscal office
• Proactively plans for upcoming internal and external meetings (set-up, agenda, catering, visitor access, parking, etc.); prepares background information and ensures timely and strategic follow up on action items; researches and resolves issues and problems without direction; assesses inquiries and concerns directed to the EVP's office, determining course of action and delegating to appropriate person to manage and uses substantial judgment and independent decision-making authority to assist with operations and maintains a high level of discretion in the handling of confidential matters.
• Identify, develop, and implement continuous process improvements to increase the efficiency and effectiveness of the EVP and the department.
• Works closely with other departments and EVP to keep him well informed of upcoming commitments and responsibilities, following up appropriately. Act as a "barometer" having a sense of the issues taking place in the organization and keeping the team updated.
• Anticipate EVP's needs in advance of any calls, meetings, trips, etc.

Responsibilities:
• Manages executive administrative level tasks to aid in the success of the EVP & Chief Revenue Officer and any direct reports; manages and processes confidential and sensitive correspondence; manages complex calendar to determine strategic use of EVP's time.
• Interacts with a wide variety of internal and external audiences, including high-level leadership, ownership, staff and external service providers while scheduling appointments, meetings and travel; coordinates itineraries and travel arrangements; serves as communications liaison with internal and external partners and develops materials for communications uses (both electronic and traditional); prepares and submits financial paperwork such as reimbursements and expense requests to the fiscal office
• Proactively plans for upcoming internal and external meetings (set-up, agenda, catering, visitor access, parking, etc.); prepares background information and ensures timely and strategic follow up on action items; researches and resolves issues and problems without direction; assesses inquiries and concerns directed to the EVP's office, determining course of action and delegating to appropriate person to manage and uses substantial judgment and independent decision-making authority to assist with operations and maintains a high level of discretion in the handling of confidential matters.
• Identify, develop, and implement continuous process improvements to increase the efficiency and effectiveness of the EVP and the department.
• Works closely with other departments and EVP to keep him well informed of upcoming commitments and responsibilities, following up appropriately. Act as a "barometer" having a sense of the issues taking place in the organization and keeping the team updated.
• Anticipate EVP's needs in advance of any calls, meetings, trips, etc.

"Assistants" "Coordinators" and that kind of thing are hard jobs to clearly define. Although it might be "fun" to work for the local basketball team, it is highly likely that this job would be terrible. You're going to do a lot of gofer work.

The definition of whether or not you did your job is dependent on the "VP of Revenue" who is the guy who runs the home games and sales. You could find yourself holding hands with Harry the Hawk while talking to third graders, and the next day, serving coffee to the NBA commissioner and a lot of famous people. You have accountability, but may not have any authority. We'll talk about accountability and authority at some point later on too.

It is very likely that the measurement of "success" in this job will be how few people on a given night will get mad at you. It is highly likely that through the eyes of some high dollar customer, this person will not do their job at some point.

Oh yeah, all of the games are at night. That could be difficult.

Another clue is that as I am writing this, the start of the NBA season is only about three weeks away, and the team still hasn't found a candidate.

## Marketing Coordinators

Ironically, in my opinion working with hundreds of companies at all levels and descriptions, this job is one of the least easy to define. No one can really tell what a "marketing coordinator" does, nor the difference between a good one and a bad one.

This one is for a "confidential" company near me.

What does that mean? It means that the person in that job right now is about to get fired, and/or the employer is fishing around in the marketplace for "just the right person."

Job duties include (but not limited to
- Study and research market trends and our competitors
- Create and execute promotional content via web and print
- Create, coordinate, and launch new products to the market
- Coordinate any and all marketing strategies and projects
- Coordinate and execute trade shows and events
- Social Media Marketing
- Coordinate and conduct product trainings for new and existing customers
- Network and collaborate with influential industry professionals to further promote our products
- Provide exceptional customer service via phone, email, social media, and trade shows/events.
- Lead generation

Required:
- Highlight organized, proactive, and forward thinking
- Some travel (domestic and international). Less than 20%
- Overtime work when necessary and needed
- Some college or college degree
- Proven and previous marketing experience in the same or similar position
- 3 professional references
- Microsoft Office
- Mac or Windows platform experience
- In office: Monday - Friday / 9am - 5pm
- Profit-driven
- Self-sufficient and multi-task projects & duties
- Provide exceptional customer service and be well-spoken
- Have a creative mind and imagination
- Have an eye for detail
- Meet deadlines
- Team player

I'd have to say that this is the exact type of job that the person in it would say that they don't know what their job is. There is a requirement for being "well spoken," whatever that is.

The job pays $50K a year, and you'll be expected to drop everything in your personal life and travel internationally at the whim of the boss, who is some high-level marketing person.

I'd also have to say this job is highly susceptible to burnout, the measurement of success is ill-defined, and is highly dependent on whether the boss "likes you", with all of the underlying baggage associated with that. The words "attractive female" do not appear on here anywhere, but you know, there may be an unstated, underlying expectation.

I pick on marketing people all the time because I was one for a while.

## Reasons for People Not Knowing What their Job Is

Now that we've seen a few examples of jobs that people are not likely to know what are, we can have a discussion about why this happens. I have narrowed this down to three reasons: The "accidental job", scope creep, aka "superheroism" and management laziness.

## The Accidental Job

This happens a lot in startup companies. A manager, it is usually a manager, gets overloaded with work. He or she then hires an assistant of some kind to help out. What are they helping out with? Well, that's up to the manager.

It is very uncommon for people in this type of situation to spend a lot of time on analyzing their job, and making a determination of exactly what duties they want to offload. So, they create a position, and come up with a job description, not knowing exactly how this employee will spend their time, and the exact skills needed. Also, once this person gets hired, there may even be some resistance on the part of the boss to give up some responsibility thinking that it will make him or her more vulnerable.

You can actually do a search of "newly created positions" if you want.

Here's an example:

**Job description**

ASSISTANT CONTROLLER ASSISTANT CONTROLLER - Newly created position at one of Denver's top real estate companies! One of Denver's top real estate companies is looking for an experience real estate accounting professional to their incredible staff! The company strives to create a fun, family-focused, honest and energetic environment! We are seeking a degreed accountant, CPA preferred and 5-7 years of progressive experience required.
Real estate experience is required.
YARDI, Paycom, Nexus and Concur experience a plus.
RESPONSIBILITIES OF THE ASSISTANT CONTROLLER Assist in the completion of the monthly, quarterly, and annual close process of multiple properties to meet reporting deadlines to financial partners.
Assist in the completion of the monthly, quarterly, and annual joint venture accounting and reporting requirements.
Compile lender requirements to assist with lender reporting compliance.
Ensure monthly debt service payments are funded and recorded.
Manage the bi-weekly processing of payroll.
Actively manage labor allocations via payroll application, record the allocation of payroll costs and transfer funds accordingly from each property.
Prepare 401(k) data transfer and Manage the 401(k) function Prepare quarterly Real Estate Owned report.

Note the couple of grammatical errors in the job description. This looks like an accountant for a real estate management company.

There are multiple properties, they need to come up with a set of financial statements every month to inform their partners, and there needs to be someone who does payroll. That implies that there are a lot of employees of one kind or another.

What you're going to be doing is spending a lot of time chasing down employees that didn't do their paperwork properly, or property managers whose books are screwed up. You're also at the whim of the boss, who is at the whim of his or her boss.

## Do you know what your job is?

It's possible that you'd be dealing with an accounting system that might or might not already be a mess. You suspect that the Controller was overloaded, or they wouldn't be looking for an assistant. There are some negative ramifications on you as well. Depending on what your boss is like, it is possible that you could end up in jail, ref: Alan Weisselberg.

I don't know what type of employee they hope to get. The salary is $25 an hour, so around $50K a year, and the prospective employee with 5-7 years of experience is likely to have his or her hands full.

I am not pointing any fingers; it is possible that the management thought this through carefully and did a good job of describing this. But it is also possible that this job happened by accident, has not been thought out, and the new employee, a CPA, will not know what their job is.

The average salary of a CPA in Denver is $118K per year. That's another thing they could have thought through a little better.

## Scope Creep aka "Superheroism"

I have been in a dozen places where there are "superheroes." This is a person with his or her (it is more often a "her") tentacles in several of the processes and functions of the business. Very often, this is a scheduler or some other employee like that, who is so good at their job that they accumulate more and more responsibility.

If you want to find out what is going on in a place, you talk to them.

In fact, this is a deliberate career strategy. There is an article in the references that talks about how to make yourself indispensable around the place. More often this happens by accident, because the boss finds out that worker is efficient, conscientious, dependable, creative, and gets their job done with a minimum of flak.

A lot of people pick up additional responsibility in their work. That's a desirable characteristic of a "team player" in a way.

What happens is, that over a period of time, a worker will eventually reach their limit of taking on more responsibility. At that point, the organization is vulnerable, isn't it?

At some point, it is even possible that the superhero will turn into super villain. He or she will start to possess inside knowledge that even the managers of the organization don't know. At that point the management actually loses ownership. I have a couple of stories on how this actually happened.

Organizational Knowledge

https://www.youtube.com/watch?v=Ld002TJ3Ovc

## Going Rogue

It's actually more likely that one of these superheroes eventually goes rogue and quits, or retires, and takes that knowledge with them. You'd be surprised at how many times I've seen a superhero quit, and have to be replaced by two or three people.

Therefore, it's best, from a management point of view, to recognize and put some controls on it.

## Preventing Scope Creep

The "Agile" people have this figured out. Agile is a software development environment, and a lot of companies have gone to it. In Agile, there is such a thing as a "sprint" which is a two-week program of people doing their jobs.

The "scrum master", who is typically the project manager, assigns tasks to different members of the team which he or she expects to fill up the two-week period for each of the team members. This keeps everybody on task, and keeps everyone busy.

The "scrum master" eventually gets good at figuring out how many person-days a given task will take, which is a benefit of the system.

But the whole thing depends on discipline. Everybody in the system, including the management, has to agree to honor the sprint and not load their tasks into the system randomly without removing a task of the same size from the developer's plate. That way there's no such thing as overloading someone, there is agreement on prioritization of projects, and the system works.

So that's the solution for "regular companies." At some point, the management has to be alert to the existence of superheroes, and avoid giving them additional work that will ultimately burn them out. That would require management to be aware of peoples' job activities, and in some organizations that's a bit of a stretch.

Here's another video. The short version is, someone has to tell the "senior stakeholder" "NO."

Scope Creep Scrum Master

https://youtu.be/MXVIGZwK12s?si=C1qL4Q4CQGfz7A6v/

## Management Laziness

The final reason for the issuance of poor job descriptions is resistance or laziness on the part of the hiring manager.

A lot of managers hate taking time to do job analyses, particularly in startups or family businesses. This is because it is an overhead activity that a lot of hiring managers prefer not to do. Is this "laziness?" I would never accuse a manager of being lazy.

The second part of this is that managers want to be able to pile more work onto someone. They want the flexibility of increasing the workload. Is it "fair" for an employee to be hired based on one set of expectations, and then have a lot of extra responsibility dumped on them? In most professionally run organizations, this is considered not beneficial.

This is one of the things that union contracts were invented to prevent, when it comes right down to it.

In reality, the boss doesn't respect the work. They haven't taken the time to understand a lot of the work that is going on in their own departments. This is a further can of worms when there are reorganizations, or buyouts and a new boss joins the team and needs to figure out who is doing what. If job descriptions and position content documents are developed randomly and not updated, employees find themselves doing work that doesn't matter to anyone. That reduces employee motivation, and increases disengagement.

And, since this is also linked to performance evaluations and pay scales, there is some incentive for some budget-sensitive bosses to give the whole thing a thumbs down.

## People Don't Know What Their Jobs Are

A primary reason that people don't do their jobs is that people don't know what their job is. Only one in three employees know their role in the organization.

There are several underlying reasons for this, starting from before the point at which the employee is hired. Jobs aren't well thought out, nor are the measurements of success. Scope creep may potentially overload employees. All of these things can be prevented by management effort, but managers sometimes do not respect the job, and don't put in the effort.

Clearly defined roles and expectations are critical to job satisfaction, employee retention, and productivity.

Links and References

https://youtu.be/az2GjRBXTN0

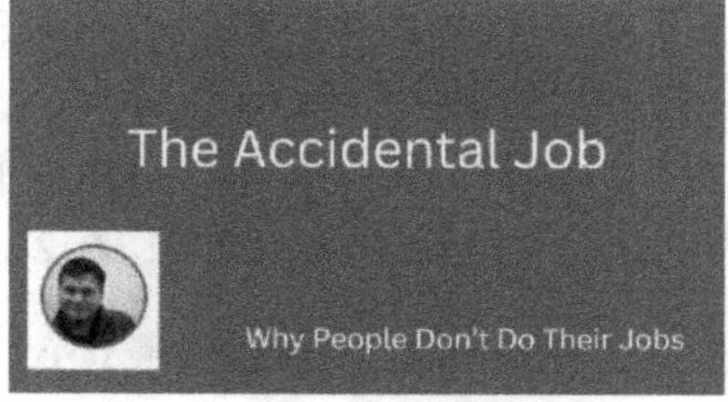

# 06 Entrenched Mediocrity

Entrenched Mediocrity is the answer to the "next question." We talked in the introduction about the "five why" method of root cause analysis. This book was written because of the idea that people do a lot of analysis and come up with "human error" as the solution. But, accepting that, they still do not fix the problem.

Or, to put it a different way, you know there's a problem, you know the solution, why didn't you fix it?

There are the four working definitions of "Entrenched Mediocrity."

*An obvious beneficial change is resisted, especially for non-technical reasons*

*The organization accepts mediocrity to avoid the cost of change*

*A widely known problem is allowed to continue despite obvious risk*

*Overhead activities become more important than production*

A given organizational issue can have elements of more than one of these definitions, by the way. In fact, that is the more common situation.

## More about Mediocrity

We know all about mediocrity.

There is plenty in the literature about being ordinary and hating it, but a lot of people, organizations and nations are ordinary and like it that way.

It's not necessarily evil, but it is a loss of human potential. Also, as we're about to see, it's temporary. There is a law of physics that is sucking you downward as an organization.

We also know about being entrenched. This is about a sufficiently well-established and deep-rooted condition. Often it is human, but it doesn't have to be. It isn't "immovable" per se. With some amount of effort, a well-established piece of concrete can be blasted out. But there is often a significant effort involved.

That being the case, there are four specific definitions for Entrenched Mediocrity

## Change Resistance for Non-Technical Reasons

I have an example of this in this little video that I did a few years ago:

https://youtu.be/Lc9a-J2RmhQ

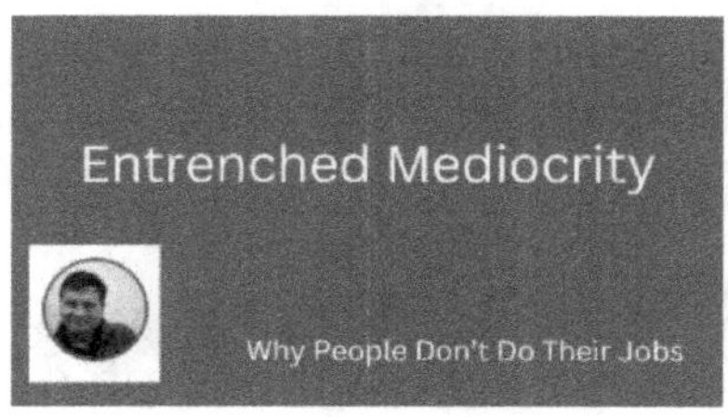


I myself didn't do my job of checking a box, because the box scrolled off the top of my screen when I uploaded a few documents. It wasn't just me. This was a common failure mode, and a lot of people in the organization I was in were doing the same thing.

That would make it a systemic problem.

So, a systemic problem usually requires that some system be changed in order to solve it. But in this case, a big organization, it was utterly impossible to get that level of change done, even though the creation of an error trap or other method is fast and easy.

The organization may have its reasons for not doing the change. This is IT related, and IT activities are notorious for this. The IT department is typically overworked, and in a lot of places it is work like resetting peoples' passwords and hand holding, and once the change is made, they have to be able to roll it out to X number of thousands of remote viewers. The software itself was developed "pre-cloud" thus making it a "legacy system."

We're going to talk about technostress a little later.

To make a long story short, the immediate short-term solution was determined to be "beat on the victim" rather than solve the problem.

## Avoiding the Cost of Change

In this definition, mediocrity is accepted to avoid the cost of change. I believe we can all think of examples of this in our personal and work lives.

If you want an example, you can look at the famous episode of the GM vehicles whose ignition switch shut off while driving, particularly if the driver had a lot of heavy stuff attached to the key ring.

The problem was known for a long time, and attributed to a cheap plastic part, the cost of which was estimated by Time Magazine as less than $1 per car.

The cost to fix the ignition switches was estimated to be about $350 per car.

The problem was known for about a decade before anything was done about it, and the company accepted the risk to avoid the cost of re-engineering the part, which could have been done cheaply.

Car recalls happen all the time. The company accepted a part that worked in a mediocre fashion to avoid the cost of changing it. A further argument is that they knew the risk and accepted it. We're going to talk about that later, but it is very common.

## Risk Acceptance

There is an element of risk acceptance in a lot of these examples.

In this definition, a widely known problem is allowed to continue despite obvious risk. There doesn't have to be cost, or anyone's feelings involved, but there can be.

Here's my favorite example.

I was given the opportunity at one point to improve the profitability of a little processing operation. In this operation, there was a big propane furnace, a process input which was a bit annoying, and a process output which was also a bit annoying but less so.

The furnace itself was developed by a fellow who I knew personally. He lived out the dream that some of us have of inventing something and then turning it into a commercially successful venture. At one point, he hired a "gofer" who worked beside him to learn the process.

At some later point, the process was sold to an Angel Investor, and the founder retired. The Gofer was hired to be the plant manager, since he knew how to run the process. At about that time, a second plant, also founded by the inventor, blew up and killed a lot of people. So, it was recognized that the process itself was dangerous, and you had to know what you were doing to run it.

## The Plot Thickens

So, my job in this was, as an employee of the Angel Investor, to go in, get information about how to run the system, and if possible, make improvements. A side complication was that this place was about 300 miles away at the time, and the idea was hatched at the possibility of moving it.

The Gofer/plant manager was big, profane and rude, and at one point threatened me physically. Since he was also well known to be carrying firearms, I did what I could to get some information, and reported it back to the organization. Come to find out that he was doing the same thing to everybody, even the owners of the company.

After I did a few calculations, I found out that the process itself was about 2% thermodynamically efficient, that is to say, based on the amount of propane used and the heat generated, 98% of the fuel cost was going up the stack as waste heat.

Not long after that, the UPS driver that went to that place reported to the company the suspicion that the employee was selling and using illegal drugs out of the plant. Heaven is High, and the Emperor is Far Away, as the saying goes.

The obvious risks were: Only one person knew how to "safety" run a dangerous process. That person was also at risk to be busted for drug sales, and probable use.

I have been in this sort of situation a number of times over the years, and the most professionally run organizations fire everybody involved, and if need be close the place down. This organization chose to accept both of these risks, and continue to operate at 2% efficiency. There was a cost consideration, and also the consideration of the cost of walking away.

I believe this sort of thing happens all the time. A trusted employee has a drug or alcohol problem, and doesn't get fired, and no one wants to walk away from some sunk cost, despite the fact that someone might be killed.

## Overhead Activities

The last of these definitions involve overhead activities. Overhead activities are prioritized over production.

I have a funny video on this, too:

https://youtu.be/rd3Ygnb__TA

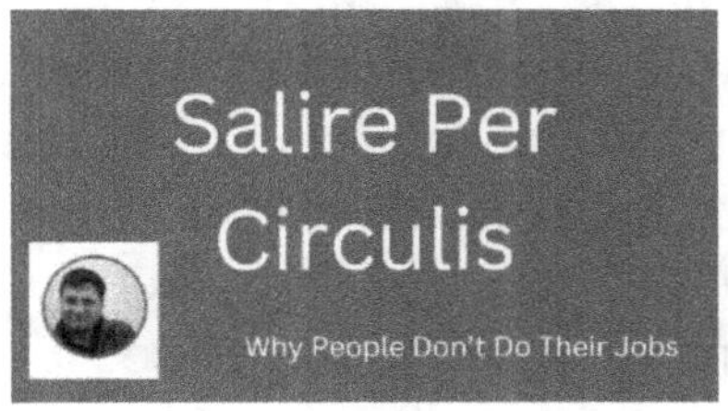


The Roman Empire took 900 years to build, and 80 years to destroy. I will let you study the causes of the collapse of the Roman Empire, but I think it was this: The population was too preoccupied with bureaucracy, religion, and sporting events to realize that an army carrying spears and rocks was about to sack it.

I will let you do further research on the character Tom Peters, who did a lot of work back in the 1980's on "excellence."

He tells the story of Nucor Steel, who back in the 1980's was one of the pioneers of the strategy of small and agile, and capturing small markets. The idea they had was "flattening the layers" in that there were only four levels of organization between the CEO and the plant floor. In order to accomplish that, there had to be a conscious management decision to limit the size of the manufacturing facilities.

In my opinion, as someone who has been in more than a hundred companies, including startups and huge corporations and everyplace between, there are two critical times in the development of an organization.

## Lessons from Startups

One is, when the organization reaches about 15 people. That's roughly the number of people that an entrepreneur can boss around in one day. Any more than that makes it too hard for one person to monitor. Above that number, the boss has to develop and implement processes and procedures, and as we are going to see later, that isn't easy. It requires a different skillset from the one that started the company in the first place.

Another is when they reach about 100 people. The above fellow from Nucor, Ken Iverson, identified that number as the point at which people stop talking to each other. The communication processes become too complicated, and problem solving becomes more difficult.

There is actually some recent research to the effect that the human brain can only process a community of about 150 people, without having issues. I am not ready to quibble about whether the number is 100 or 150.

It's also the point, by the way, at which "the overhead" can make a career out of saying "no." I worked for a place for a while in which about ⅓ of the technical management of the place literally built a career out of rejecting research and development activities.

I will let you figure out how this works in the work organizations you are involved in, but to make a long story short, if an organization gets to be so big and so old that it a career may be made by killing opportunities, that's not good.

Ken Iverson himself passed away in 2002, but according to the article which I have linked the organizational structure is still flat and decentralized. Their earnings have gone from about $200 million, since 2002, to $9.7 Billion today, and earnings per ton from $42 to $400 in that time period.

## Resistance

The writer Stephen Pressfield has come up with the concept of Resistance, which we will talk about later.

Resistance is defined as the universal force that keeps things the same. He sees this in his context as a writer. Resistance is the force that keeps writers from writing, painters from painting, and organizations from organizing. It accepts people living in a van down by the river.

But, as he points out, it only works in one direction. Resistance keeps people and organizations and nations from getting to a higher form of existence. But it does not keep them from getting worse. There is a universal force, entropy that will pull you, your organization, and your society downward if you let it.

So that's the danger of Entrenched Mediocrity. At some point, it leads to organizational decline and collapse, if it is permitted to continue.

Maybe that's why I am writing this. My contribution to the enhancement of humankind. I'm trying to keep that from happening.

## Entrenched Mediocrity

Here is your project: As we go through some of these examples, of "why people don't do their jobs" and why some of these things happened, think of them all as some artifact of the four types of 'entrenched mediocrity."

It won't necessarily help anyone change it, but at least you'll understand that mediocrity is endemic to the human condition, and is very difficult to overcome.

Links and References

# 07 Accountability and Authority

We're going to talk about accountability and authority now. The reason for this is to try to understand a little better whether or not people are going to do their jobs, based on where they are in whatever system they're in, and why it matters.

We're going to put them all on a graph, so we can understand it a little better, and then we're going to introduce some concepts.

This isn't really academic. It's to get you, the reader, to understand why it's really hard to get some people to do their jobs. Here's the list:

| **Employee** | **Accountability (Customer Intimacy)** | **Authority (Empowerment to fix problems)** |
|---|---|---|
| Machinist | Minimal (not zero) | Minimal (not zero) |
| Janitor in the same factory | None | None |
| Plant manager in the same factory | Medium (Less than the sales department) | Medium (May be limited by corporate structure) |

| | | |
|---|---|---|
| Corporate Big Shot (Machining Company) | Little or none | Organizationally greater than the plant manager but not maximum. |
| Airline Pilot | Maximum | Maximum (Licensed by the Government) (System Limited) |
| Airline flight attendant | Maximum | Not as high as the pilot (System limited) |
| Airline Bag Handler (outsourced) | None | None |
| Airline big shot | Minimal | Fairly high, but limited by legacy systems |
| Fast Food Worker | Maximum | Minimal, but not zero |
| Fast Food Store Manager | Very high but less than the window worker | Some but limited by franchise agreement. |
| Fast Food Marketing Coordinator (Corporate) | Depends on the customer (May be intimate with internal | None (Limited to knowledge transfer) or Strategic |

| | | |
|---|---|---|
| | customers) | |
| Celebrity Chef | High ("Chef" is part of the product) | High (Can scream at kitchen staff) |
| Massage Therapist | Less than pilot, but very high | Maximum (Licensed by the government) |
| White Collar Criminal | None | Maximum |
| Supervillain | None | Maximum |
| "The Amorphous They" | (May be intimate with internal customers) | Somewhere between none and very high. Probably not the same as Supervillain or White-Collar Criminal. No one knows who they are, but they are often to blame for stupid decisions and policies for that reason. |

## Manufacturing Model

Let's consider a machinist in a big corporate machine shop. I've been in several of these. Normally, in these places, there are big computerized cutting machines (CNC machines) and elsewhere in the plant there's an assembly operation that puts together whatever the assembly is. The one I am thinking of at the moment was in Oklahoma, and the machining and assembly operations make a football-sized hydraulic pump.

Accountability, in this case, is the tendency to be "blamed" personally for any problems that happen with the product, and "authority" is the empowerment and level of control that the employee has to fix something.

The machinist we are talking about is at the lower left. They never see a customer, and have no ability other than to fix a small scale screw-up to either help or hurt the customers. He didn't design the part, he's not going to install it into the assembly, once it leaves his very limited work station, he's done with it and onto the next.

He may have some internal customers, such as the quality control inspector and/or his supervisor to deal with, but for the most part, he's on his own.

Is he or she likely to do his job? Well, this is measurable, in terms of "defect rate." Somewhere greater than 95% of the time, the system works.

Next, we're going to consider the janitor in the same factory, who may or may not be outsourced. He has no external customer intimacy at all, and no external accountability at all. If he has any accountability, it's to his internal customer, namely his supervisor, who presumably catches wind of it if he (it is less likely to be a male) goes into a dark corner and takes a nap.

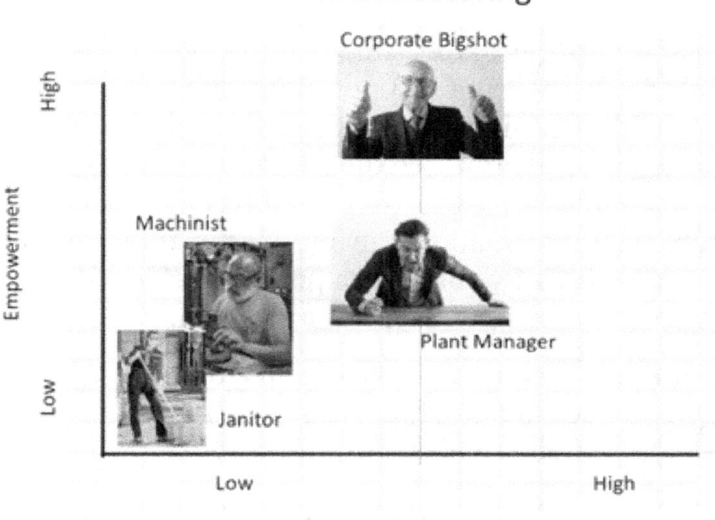


## Accountability and Authority

What I'm saying is that because of where these two employees are in this system, it's hard to get them to do their jobs. In each of the above two cases, they're a long way from any external customer, and they're limited in their empowerment to doing what they are told.

In the case of the machinist, they've computerized his equipment to increase the chances of him doing his job properly.

The machinist may or may not catch hell from a hard headed supervisor occasionally, but for the most part, as long as the equipment is functioning properly, there will be controlled conditions. In fact, since he gets his hands on the product he is likely to be highly trained, thus making him even more able to do his job than the janitor working next to him.

The plant manager in the same plant is more empowered. In most modern corporate operations, he or she is in contact with the sales function, directly or indirectly. He or she is also able to influence the employees and local political people, solve problems, and fix customer issues, if they are related to manufacturing. The customer in the case I was thinking about was a producer of little construction vehicles that the pumps are installed onto.

Since there is customer accountability, and also some ability to make changes, the plant manager in this place is more empowered. That's your "authority figure."

There may or may not be a corporate big shot in the same company. He or she may be involved with the sales effort, communicates frequently with the plant manager, and has external customers, namely the owners or stockholders of the company to deal with. He is less intimate with the end users, but more intimate with the tycoons and financiers that are the investors. His job, as a manager, is to maximize the wealth of the shareholders.

You know that show "Undercover Boss?" This is where they take a corporate big shot, and make him or her work as a burger flipper or some otherwise low level and/or customer facing person. The reason it is interesting is the idea that these people commonly lose touch with what is actually going on in the operations.

## The Airline Model

The airline model is a little different. In the airlines, the most highly trained person in the system is the pilot. This person, it is usually a male, used to be mainly military in terms of background, but now we're told that only about ½ or less of these pilots have had military experience.

But, as a pilot you need to have a commercial pilot training course, satisfy requirements for flight hours, get instrument certification, and be around for a while. Therefore there is a financial barrier in this for people as well.

It is so important for us, as a society, to have commercial pilots that do their jobs, that the government requires them to be licensed, and there are legal consequences if you show up at your job loaded.

These people are also intimate with their customers in that whatever happens to the customers also happens to them. There are a couple of cases in the last few years of pilots flipping out on the job, and taking the passengers with them on a one-way trip, if you know what I mean.

So, in our graph of accountability and authority, they're way at the upper right, except to say that even pilots are the focal point of a huge complex system of maintenance, and training and infrastructure, so they're not completely empowered.

Lower on the right is going to be the flight attendant on the same plane. This person is actually more customer facing than the pilot, and has a complicated job. They need to help efficiently load the plane, including all of those little old ladies that can't lift their carryon bag into the overhead compartment, the overweight person that needs a seat belt extension, and any number of wailing infants and drunk partygoers.

They also have to perform important safety checks, and are responsible for managing the process of emergency evacuation.

They also have to keep an eye on the shifty ones, and make sure there is no funny business on the plane, and no one likes to think about that.

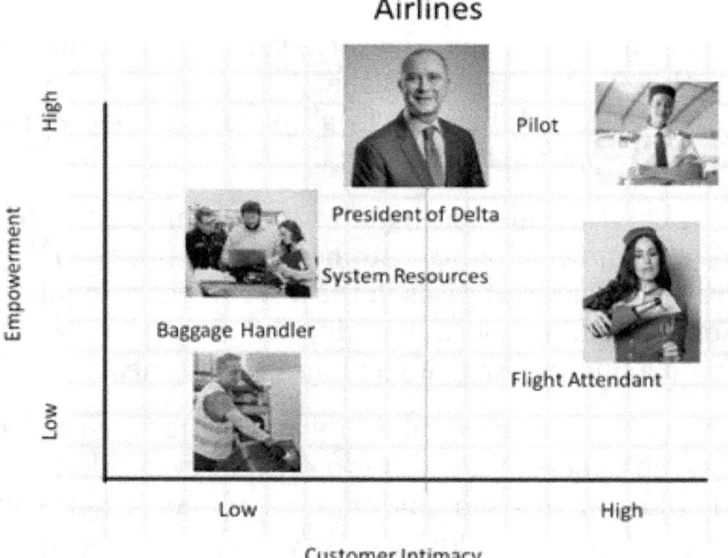


## Flight Attendant Authority

The flight attendant has some authority, however. Flight attendants are considered federal agents, and if you refuse to cooperate with a flight attendant, you're violating federal law.

So, in a way, that makes them more empowered than the drunk plant manager of the manufacturing facility that staggers into the plane after the company golf outing.

Side note: Drunk flying is not pleasant, but some people still do it.

In the airline industry, there are also corporate bigshots and low wage employees. The low wage employees would be the baggage handlers and restroom cleaners. These people make $15 an hour and have to lift bags at midnight on the runway in Cleveland, in December. Nowadays, a lot of these employees are working for subcontractors and outsourcing entities, rather than directly with the airlines.

There is a collection of gate agents, customer service people, and IT brainiacs that keep the very complicated reservations and ticketing systems functioning, as well as a lot of mechanics and other support personnel.

The corporate bigshots are the most highly paid people in the system and know the least about flying or baggage handling. They, like the corporate bigshots in manufacturing, very often enter the industry through the financial system or other means.

According to his bio, the President of Delta graduated from college in the field of finance. He worked his way up through the "airline industry" but it is unlikely he ever landed a plane, threw a bag onto a belt with snow coming down in Cleveland, or cleaned out an airline restroom.

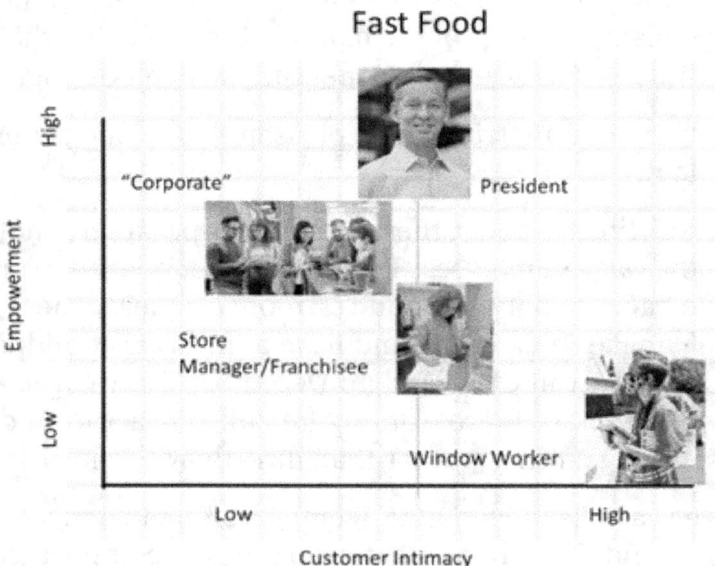


## The Retail Fast Food Model

So now you get the picture. Let's apply it to retail fast food.

You have a fast-food worker. Let's make it the window worker at your favorite drive through. That poor person has the misfortune of being the most customer facing member of a vast, complex system. If the customer doesn't get what they want, or doesn't like their food, it's them that usually catches hell.

Their customer accountability is therefore the maximum possible, equal to or more than the airline pilot, and comparable to the flight attendant.

By the way, what's the "defect rate?" How often is a customer's order screwed up? Well unless he or she is having a bad day, an order is correctly filled around 92% of the time, which is actually not that much worse than our factory guy up above. At Panera, probably because of order complexity, about 1 in 5 orders has an error. The reason the success rates are that high in fast food is that the menu has limited complexity, and there are other systems in place to make sure our window person puts the right thing in the bag.

Tom Peters, management talking head from the 80's points out correctly that the most customer facing member of any complex system gets the least amount of respect. In education, it's the teachers. In the phone company, it's the service person in India. In the airlines, it's the flight attendant and in fast food, it's that person at the window.

They're also the person in the system least empowered to solve a problem. They're not federal agents. They can't go back and fix anything that the kitchen has sent them. If they screw up, and pour you the wrong drink, they're empowered in the moment to fix it.

They can't get people to show up for work. They aren't to blame if there's no such thing as a 3/8 pounder.

In our proverbial graph of accountability and authority, they're way down at the lower right.

Their boss, the store manager, is still customer facing most of the time, but still not all that empowered to solve processing problems, can't put new things on the menu, and is limited in his ability to enact change.

Here's a funny video about the McDonalds ice cream machines. These gadgets are down 34% of the time due to limitations on where they can get spare parts. This is not because the parts are complicated, but because of contractual agreements that are depriving us of our ice cream.

McDonalds Ice Cream Machines

https://www.youtube.com/watch?v=2uCpY3tFTI

## The Franchisees

In this system there is such a thing as an "owner operator". The person that "owns" the store. Another word for this is the franchisee. In the case of McDonalds, this person, is screened by having a net worth of up to $500,000 per year, and subject to a lot of other restrictions. It is not completely unheard of for one franchisee to own several of these stores.

The franchisees are empowered to run the operations, but not empowered to introduce new menu items, or change the store appearance or location, or make any changes at all because of contracts with the main office.

Above that, there are corporate employees for the companies that make a lot of these decisions and select the franchisees, and decide what toy goes into the Happy Meals. They also define and control the "franchisee experience." They very often come from other industries and have never flipped a burger. In the case of the McDonalds, the CEO went to Duke and the Harvard Business School, and started out in "consumer products" like Kraft and PepsiCo.

He may have been forced to flip a burger or two at McDonalds' University, but it is unlikely he ever cleaned out the ice cream machine.

So, who, in this system is unlikely to do their jobs? First of all, as we will explain further on, employees at all levels will not do their jobs. The customer facing employee frequently does not do his or her job, but the consequences of an individual failure are relatively small.

## Corporate Big Shots

In all of these industries, there are "Corporate Big Shots."

Maybe you are one of these people. If so, congrats. Some people strive to be where you are.

There is a system of corporate employees, one notch down from corporate officers, and high-level managers. These people are the strategic decision makers that do things like understand and focus on core competencies, do budgeting, work with the financiers and stockholders, and in general run the business at a high level.

In this day and age, there are "skills" and "theories" that can be learned to help them do this, and "business schools" for this purpose. They get interviewed by TV talking heads sometimes. Maybe one of them will see this.

In family-owned businesses, or small businesses, there are few if any corporate bigshots. The President of the company does all of this, and may or may not have the "skills" required to run their business, which is quite often why these people don't do their jobs.

## Technocrats

At a level below the big shot level, roughly the same as the plant manager for empowerment, there are technocrats. These are technical or scientific people or engineers that design the products and otherwise develop systems that make things work, we hope. They also don't do their jobs some fraction of the time, often with hilarious results. Assemblies are designed where the bolts don't fit into the holes. Machines break down. Your car is recalled. This is sometimes due to this layer in the organization not doing its job.

This layer is why you can't talk to a human and get put on hold for 60 minutes when your mutual fund ID gets hacked.

There is sometimes a path from this level to being a corporate bigshot. As we will see later, there is often a path for these people to develop an idea and try to live out the American Dream in a startup situation.

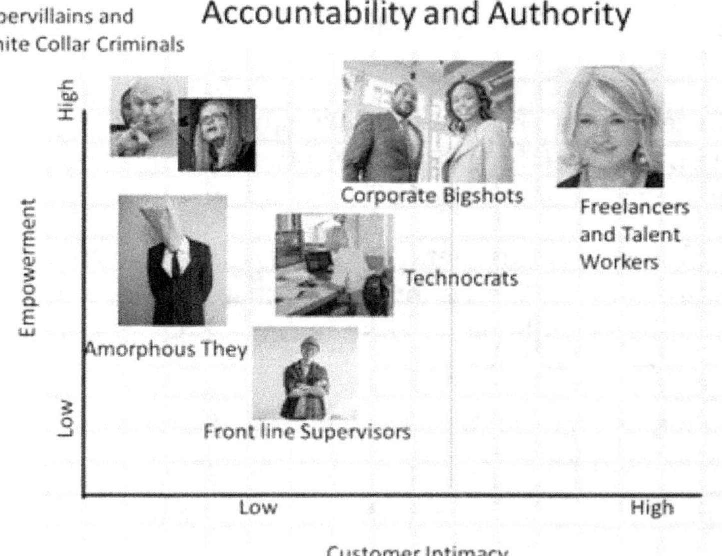


## Freelancers and "Talent Workers"

There are fewer of these people, but they have high levels of customer intimacy and also empowerment. In fact, they themselves are part of the product.

One of the best books I ever read on this topic was "How to Make $100,000 a year as a Massage Therapist" by Megan R. Holub. This describes the whole idea of incorporating the person into the product, and marketing to high-end customers.

In massage, there is a franchise outfit, Massage Envy, which is the opposite of that. In my area they pay their employees on average about $33 per hour. These would be the "hands on" retail level employees that are the equivalent of the window worker that is customer facing.

They need to be licensed by the state, to maintain health regulations and know the rules.

Does that mean they make $70,000 a year? No, it doesn't, because they can't work 40 hours a week. They only work when people want massages, and they're in competition with the massage person in the next office.

But, if you target high-end customers, are focused on customer service, and enhance the customer service experience (legally) you can sometimes do a lot better as a freelancer.

Plastic Surgeons, NFL players and Gordon Ramsey all have made a lot of money doing exactly that same thing. Do they do their jobs? Very reliably, because they are part of the product.

Me? Yes, I fall into this group too. I have, however, flipped a burger, cleaned a nasty factory floor, run a metal lathe, and was involved in a lot of other craziness from a product quality standpoint, and have some stories to tell. I've also been in some snooty board rooms, on top of the Great Wall, and have seen a lot of people who don't do their jobs, and some who do. That's what qualifies me to walk around in any factory in the world and spot some screw-up, if I am not sleep deprived from the flight.

Truthfully, I am more of a freelance technocrat. "Talent" is a bit generous in my case.

Can a talent level person become a corporate bigshot? Yes, this also happens. Joanna Gaines is one of these, as is Magic Johnson. Martha Stewart, who spent some time as a White-Collar Criminal, falls into this category.

## Supervillains and White-Collar Criminals

Speaking of which: In the very upper left of our diagram are Supervillains and White-Collar Criminals. These people usually come from the legitimate corporate environment, but have abandoned whatever ethical or moral principles they may have had.

They are totally empowered to manipulate their systems, and have no concern for the customers at all.

How does this happen? We can only guess, but we suspect that these people like power, dislike the need to obey moral and ethical rules, or pay taxes, and can see a shortcut. They usually started as high-end corporate bigshots, and then evolved into the twisted, evil maniacs that they are. They're constantly being chased by superheroes, but they don't care. In fact, for them, it's part of the fun.

Are they good at doing their jobs? To the extent that their jobs are to be evil geniuses, and make as many people as possible miserable, while they accumulate wealth and power, they are.

## The "Amorphous They"

These are the people with a lot of authority, but practically no accountability with regard to the customers. They're the senior level coordinators, mid-level assistants to people, and people lurking in the edges of corporate meetings who yell out what eventually becomes the established strategy.

They're not necessarily evil, but they can be. They work in vast complicated organizations, and the government, to make decisions that no specific person wants to be blamed for. They never face any consequences for stupidity.

"They" build their career by avoiding accountability. They are corporate drones. Small businesses and startups can't afford them. A company has to be big enough to support "Them."

"They"' are the reason the corporate reservations system shuts off your hotel reservation at midnight. "They" are the reason the ice cream machine can't get fixed. "They" are the ones who suggested "controlled demolition" and allow people to keep their jobs that shouldn't. "They" don't sound the alarm.

On the factory floor, "They" are to blame for a lot of mischief. Defective material put in the wrong area? "They" told me to do it. Stuff not assembled properly? "They" did that on the night shift.

"They" have no real organizational authority for the most part, but are in the room for critical decisions, and have "input" In a lot of the snooty corporate meetings. Does it pay well? Usually. "They" may have been long-time employees with a lot of knowledge, and kept around because of the "value" of their wisdom. "They" sometimes add a little value.

## Other Layers

There are other layers on this graph which consist of people not doing their jobs.

Just above the bottom layer, above the machinist and below the plant manager, there's a floor supervisor, or someone similar. These people are your trainers and schedulers and others that are trying to get the low wage people to work. A lot of times they are promoted into their jobs as we indicated earlier and have more of the culture and personal characteristics of the layer just below. That is to say they're equally likely to show up loaded, be disengaged, and not do their jobs as the low wage level.

There's the sales department. There are often sales people, and sales managers, and a sales VP. These people have some element of the talent worker, in that not just anybody is gifted in the field of personal relationships so as to be able to make sales. But that doesn't mean they're immune to not doing their jobs, and in fact, it is common. The same personality trait that makes you a good salesman, and entertaining in that function, also leads to you not do your paperwork properly.

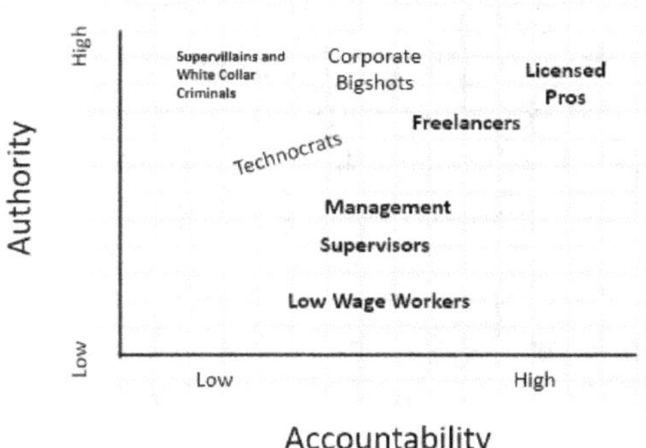


## What does any of this have to do with people not doing their jobs?

Here are the general rules of this. There are a few exceptions, in certain circumstances, but for the most part it works.

Screw-ups and people not doing their jobs happen at all of the layers.

The layer along the bottom, that would be your floor sweepers and fast-food window operators are typically low wage workers.

80% of the quality issues by "count" happen in the lowest layer, and the layer just above that, which is the supervisor layer. These screw-ups are cheap, often funny, and are an ongoing part of life. If the fraction of these screw-ups gets above about 10% (which is still 90% good) the company is vulnerable to going broke, but in some industries that number may be higher or lower under certain circumstances.

80% of the dollar amount of the screw-ups happen at the higher levels, either at the corporate bigshot layer or just below. Pilots screw up and wreck planes. Engineers screw up, and your car is recalled, along with a lot of other peoples'. The VPs of the bank screw up, and account holders are screwed over and the bank shuts down. People not doing their jobs at this level leads to process ineffectiveness and business disasters, which drives people crazy.

Among the bottom layer, there is horizontal mobility, but not vertical. It's next to impossible for someone to start as a floor sweeper and end up being a corporate bigshot nowadays. The more likely path is for these employees to move to some other company and do some other low wage job. This being the case they are the ones more likely to get loaded and/or be disengaged on the job, and not do their jobs.

At the upper levels, there is also some horizontal mobility. Corporate bigshots move from one company to another all the time. In the middle, there is less horizontal mobility because of the technical skills needed in some industries

There are entry barriers at various places in this system, the number one of which is a college degree. A young person can still skip the low wage trap and enter the workforce at a higher level with a college degree and some connections. Another one is professional licensing. Neither of these is an assurance that people won't do their jobs, but it's a start. Another is the military. People from the military are pre-screened, receive a lot of "leadership training" and have a lot of desirable skills.

The barriers between layers on this are not always intelligence, but they can be. More often, they're cultural, and no amount of education, training or experience will get through them. They require connections, and often being born to the right family. There are a few exceptions to this but it usually works out that way.

Outsourcing and temporary workers happen mainly at the low level, but also at the technical level from time to time. It's actually slightly harder to get them to do their jobs because they're slightly less engaged with the customers.

If you're reading this, we're going to assume you're either at the supervisory or technical layer. You have the misfortune of being responsible for this system being able to function, and have customers and others not go crazy.

## There you have it.

People don't do their jobs at some level because of where they are on the accountability and authority scales.

The lower you are on these two scales, the more frequently you don't do your job, but the cost of each failure is usually low. The people at the higher levels screw up more infrequently but more expensively, and more aggravatingly.

The tendency of people not to do their jobs has a significant cultural element, but education and training can partially offset this, relative to an individual person doing his or her job.

Read into this what you will. These systems have gone on since the time of the ancient people, and are not about to change.

Links and References

Why People Still Don't Do Their Jobs

https://youtu.be/euFLNLGg8p4

# 08 Starting Up is Hard to Do

In light of what we've already learned, we're going to tackle business startups now. I am not picking on anybody specifically, but I have been around a lot of this kind of business, and have a lot to say about it.

## Disclaimer

Any resemblance to any startup now or at any time in the past or future is purely coincidental except to say I have seen a dozen of them by now, and they have a lot in common. For one thing, very often, the hard headed technical guy is bald.

This is being presented for entertainment purposes only.

## Another Disclaimer

I'm going to skip over the part about starting up a nail salon or pizza place because in these businesses, people don't do their jobs and the business gets shut down for one reason: The founders are bad at math.

Anybody with a pocket calculator can back work the number of clients and/or pizzas you need to sell to cover your rent, lights, supplies and ingredients.

The main cause of business failure in these cases is that the founders haven't done those calculations and acted accordingly.

Why People Still Don't Do Their Jobs

https://youtu.be/NqkQUbFmzso

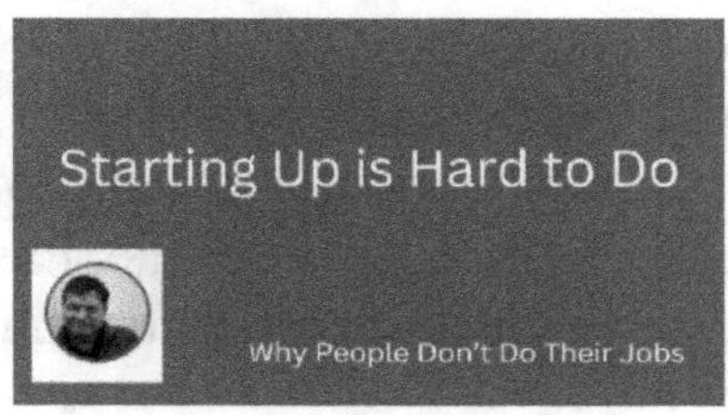


## Why People Don't Do Their Jobs: Startup Version

Let's list a few of these in the beginning. You can look for the examples as we go through the discussion.

| Reason | Description | Comments |
|---|---|---|
| 1 | Owners are "untrained" | Skill set from the corporate world does not always match reality |
| 2 | Denial | Confirmation Bias and Wishcasting |
| 3 | Processes are | Owners dislike |

| | | |
|---|---|---|
| | screwed up/minimal | "regulations" and can't capture their experience |
| 4 | Employees are disengaged | Passion decreases by 50% for each level of the business. Ownership is limited to the top level. |
| 5 | Managers are ineffective | Gofer not always effective when promoted to Manager (Peter Principle) |
| 6 | Alarm systems are ineffective | Upward communication processes are minimal or nonexistent |
| 7 | Owners are in the wrong job (the job evolves faster than the owners) | Managing complexity is the very thing the owners wanted to get away from in the first place. |
| 8 | Resource Issues | Business is chronically underfunded. Equipment is obsolete and minimally functional, ref: IT equipment. |

## The Business Startup Is Born

Here is the synopsis: A hard headed technical person, and a congenial salesman team up to start their own business.

These people are refugees from the Technocratic layer of a huge, soul draining corporation and decide to live out the American Dream. They have an idea that meets a perceived market need.

The congenial sales person runs the idea past a few possible customers, on the down-low, as does the hard headed technical person. "Great idea," they all say. Here's their org chart:

One sunny day, they decide to exit their cushy corporate jobs and open up their own shop. Will there be the need for a shop?

In this era, especially in the IT world, a lot of people don't need a shop. They can run their business out of their home office, if their product is not physical in nature.

That would make their lives a little simpler. The congenial sales person could go out and sell the product, or stay in, as the case may be. The hard headed technical person can use his or her technical gift to produce the product, and everything would be fine.

But, since we're writing the script, let's say that they don't do that. Side note: For the purposes of this, I am going to call them "he" for the moment, so wherever it says "he" below, let's say that it could equally be a "she."

## Problem 1: Paying Customers

The congenial sales person, from some cushy corporate job now has to confront reality. The skill set he developed calling on established customers no longer fits what his job is. He needs to go out and beat the bushes and develop a business. The skills he developed schmoozing the boss, and navigating office politics are now out the window.

Example: When I was in sales, briefly, I had a 20-million-pound territory, and it consisted of five customers. This was a "basic materials" business and these customers were mainly sizable corporate accounts. It was a case of managing forecasts, and doing capacity planning, and responding to customers because of people not doing their jobs.

Your congenial sales person now needs the skills of cold calling, and trying to get to the decision makers in a business. If you have never been in that situation, it is hard to explain, but we learned the other day that there are plenty of "Amorphous They" in one of these companies. These are people who like free lunches but can't actually make any decisions.

Issue one related to this fellow not doing his job is developing that skill.

Your sales person will have to weed through all of those "contacts" and his "network" and find someone in the customer's business who will say "yes."

Remember up above where I said that our two heroes went out and solicited customer feedback before they hit the road? Well, those customers either can't make a decision or are now saying "no." So, new customers will have to be found, and these customers will have to be able to pay. Until you've got inside information, you have no idea whether some of these customers have credit issues or other issues that might keep you from getting the money.

Let's give our guy some credit, and say that he gets to "yes." He found a paying customer.

## Problem 2: Creating a Product that Customers Like

So now your hard headed technical person springs into action.

In a corporate environment, he is a cog in a product development machine. There are ideas, and weeding out of ideas to find the most attractive one. There is a workshop and/or laboratory, and prototypes, and go/no go decisions. There are "Amorphous They" with market research and slide shows.

This is one of the things that stifled our hard headed technical person in that environment. There were a lot of people telling him "no." Also he was having to do a lot of work to "justify the business case" for spending time on a project.

Now, he doesn't have to do that.

He can work on a product that he thinks is fun. Let's pretend for this story that it's some kind of little electronic gadget that performs a valuable function. He "invented" this in his corporate job, but the entrenched mediocre corporate environment refused to honor it and scale it up. That happens more often than you can imagine. Part of his idea is that he can build a lot of these and sell them to the marketplace.

What if he's wrong? What if there really wasn't an opportunity? Well, there is a strong chance of this, and the fate of the business is in the balance.

## There are already several sub-problems.

First of all, the gadget has to fill an actual need, rather than a perceived need. The technical person, being hard-headed, has something called "confirmation bias" which is that if he thinks something is true, he will find data that confirms it.

Example: I am pretty sure that people want to read a book about people not doing their jobs.

One potential problem one is that the technical guy does not do his job of validating the product performance. If he or she does a poor job of this, the product will fail in the field which would be terrible.

Second of all, the predicted selling price may be distanced from reality, for a variety of reasons. For one thing, if you buy 100,000 of something, it's a lot cheaper than if you buy 10 and he has to factor that into his cost calculation for his supplies. That means he has to charge a higher price than he thought he was going to have to, which will hurt his market penetration.

Thirdly, he may find out at the end of the day that it takes him longer to build something than the technicians that worked in his old place. He may need to learn to solder.

Fourthly, he may end up with supply chain issues, and material shortages. Suppliers will often not even bother doing business with startups. In the corporate environment, there were office drones and coordinators that took care of all of those things, which takes time away from developing products. There is also some power in being "established" which the startup is not.

Then, there is the scale up problem.

## Problem 4: Scale Up Issues

So, let's say that the prototypes are successful, and our startup gets an order.

First of all, the costs and pricing need to be in line. Secondly, this had better be a "door opening" order with a potential for more business later, otherwise our sales person will have to beat the bushes some more.

And, ultimately, the market for this product had better be large enough, and profitability high enough that the business can sustain itself. There is customer credibility on the line.

And let's also say that they are small enough that any potential competition ignores them, and they can give some actual value to the marketplace that they can collect money for. Even if they give excellent service, there is a certain part of the business that will cut your throat for a few cents per part even if your service is brilliant.

So, it's one thing making one or two of these things in their garage, but now they have to scale up, and they have to have a competitive advantage in the marketplace.

There's no way that the hard headed technical person can make enough of them. Do you want your sales person coming off the road to run a soldering station? Of course not. He's your food chain.

There is a strong possibility that the startup will not do its job.

## Problem 5: The Workforce

So, they hire a gofer/assembler. Here's our new organization:

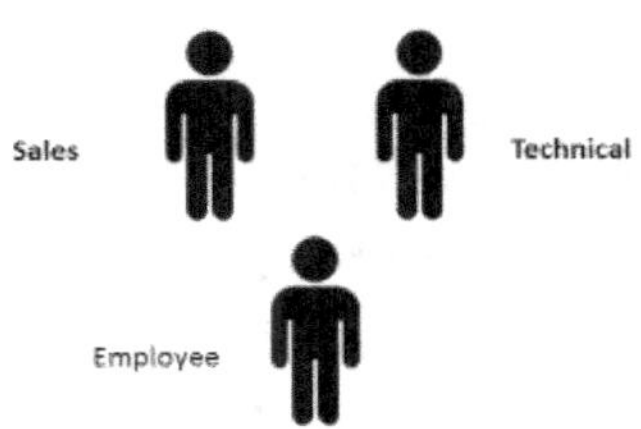


Who is this employee? At the moment they don't have technical sophistication, there is no need for the employee to be too scientific, so it's likely someone off the street.

They hire a low wage worker. The technical person trains him or her to assemble the product, and the management can go back to doing what they need to do.

Did this employee willing to leave their current job to come to work with this startup? Unlikely. It's a startup. This person came from the labor pool. Not only does our startup need to pay them, but they have to be competitive with other jobs in the area, and that includes benefits.

This employee is also not as engaged in the business as the founders, nor is he or she passionate enough to go for a long time without pay. Or "any" time.

Here's a rule: The passion in a startup decreases by 50% for each layer of employee under the management.

Also, since this is a low wage employee there is a limit to what they can do from an ability standpoint. They can't spot and solve problems, they can't make technical decisions, and they might not even understand the fundamental need to not ship junk to the customers.

## Problem 6: Cash Flow

Even if our heroes manage to produce that first big order, they are financing their material cost, rent, wages and benefits for their gofer, and keeping the lights running out of their pockets. Not to mention the fact that they haven't paid themselves a cushy corporate salary at this point.

That may be inconvenient for your former corporate people, so they might have to arrange financing. There is business planning, and presentations to investors and all of that also takes time. In the corporate world, there are professionals who do that kind of thing. But in our little startup, it's the founders and that takes time away from their actual jobs.

It also means that there is another set of eyes looking over their shoulders which is exactly the opposite of what they wanted to do in the first place.

This is unlikely to be the bank, since bankers are notoriously conservative and fearful. This is more likely to be some venture capitalist or Angel Investor. That is not all bad, but it risks some control of the business.

If you want a historical example of this, look at the case of Henry Ford, who got so mad at his Angel Investors that he decided (twice) to walk away and tell them to stick it. Much later, his heirs had to take the business public, but had to wait until long after his passing to do it literally over his cold dead body.

Yet another potential risk of the founders not doing their jobs is this whole activity of financing the business, which was not part of their cushy corporate job.

## Problem 7: Controlled Operating Conditions

Let's say that our heroes manage to navigate all of this successfully. They manage to face all of these problems plus collect their invoices and pay their suppliers. They manage to deal with their communications and personality issues without getting at each other's throats. I didn't tell you above that these two employees are the opposites, from a personality standpoint.

They may even need to navigate the issues with competition, and financing, and regulatory officials. Who knew that the EPA would inspect their little shop, which is now busting at the seams?

They'll lose that first big customer, because of someone in all of this not doing their job, but if they're really lucky maybe pick up some others.

Here's their new organization:

By this time, they have several new problems. The first one is the gofer. Do they make him or her the plant supervisor? If so, they're running exactly the same risk we talked about elsewhere. A good gofer may not make a good supervisor. The Peter Principle in action.

The workers are newly hired, and someone has to train and monitor them, or they won't do their jobs. They also have mouths to feed, and need money. They also start out as being unemployed as part of the local labor pool, whatever that looks like.

Is your supervisor a good trainer? No, it is likely he will be a bad trainer because he (correctly) fears that one of these new employees will replace him.

The technical guy also becomes a trainer and a quality control person to make sure the employees don't send junk.

And the technical guy has to respond to customer complaints when people don't do their jobs.

This is while the sales guy is presumably on the road trying to grow the business.

## Thought Question

At this point, since they now actually have to produce something, the question is re-asked: Why do they need a factory? What is value-added about hiring a workforce and making these themselves? Why don't they just hire it out to someone who is already established? Why do they have to be in North America?

Well, there are several technical and business elements to this idea. The Nike Corporation took the position that their core competency was design and marketing, and that they should not make anything. They farmed their whole manufacturing business to some crazy land.

But not everybody is Nike. A big objection is the intellectual property. If our heroes outsource the business, there is risk that whoever it is on the other end will copy the idea and it won't be proprietary anymore. That way they're competing with their own suppliers. Or, it is possible that their suppliers will do a mediocre job and the factory will be 7 time zones away with no legal system.

There are also supply chain and financing issues with subcontracting this out.

But that's not to say that it is out of the question.

There is also such a thing as "doubtsourcing" which we talked about earlier. Why don't our heroes just lease equipment, and hire a lot of "temporary" workers. There are outsourcing companies who will do the job of recruiting this labor force for them, along with administering their pay and benefits, and replacing the ones who quit.

The problem with that, of course, is that if the job requires some technical skill, the owners don't want to be constantly training a new workforce. So, you could pay the outsourcing people to do the "less value added" jobs like packaging and clean up, so that your "skilled labor force" can concentrate on producing perfect gadgets.

## Controlled Conditions

Hiring a workforce is a form of scale-up, and scale-up can't be done unless the operating procedure is completely established.

We're going to talk about operating procedures later too. It's pretty easy to screw them up.

But the main problem here is social. Your two founders, who grew to dislike operating procedures when they were in their corporate role, now have to embrace them.

If they don't, there will be a limit as to how big this business can scale up.

What I mean is a systemized set of methods, some of which may need to be documented, to be sure that these gadgets are produced equally beautifully every time. This may mean consistent supplies, consistent order of operations, and a set of known quality control standards that can be tested by a low wage workforce.

And, if you find out that some of your assemblies are screwed up because someone didn't do their job, you need to have a way to make sure none of them got out into the world.

So now you have documents and records, and potential non-conforming assemblies, and sets of rules. And, since rules are made to be broken, there need to be ramifications for any of the low wage workers who do.

So there has to be motivation, and company policies, and ways to prevent people from showing up drunk. There have to be disciplinary hearings, and investigations.

Their first case of sexual harassment may occur at about this stage.

## Problem 8: How to cope?

Our heroes are going to have to hire overhead.

Here are two rules. I have learned these by being around dozens of startup companies in all sorts of different industries. We talked about this earlier.

One rule is, that a critical point in an organization will be reached when they reach about 15 people. At that point, it's too big for your hard headed technical person to train and supervise them all. This goes double when the founders reach the point at which they can hire assistants for themselves. This would be an assistant sales manager, and an assistant technical person who will help run the plant. These are usually former corporate people who would like to get corporate level salaries.

The second rule is: the amount of passion in an organization decreases by 50% for each level below the founders. That means once the assistants are hired, at the low level, the workers have only ⅛ as much passion as the founders, which might not be noticeable for a low wage worker.

At this point, the paperwork blizzard is likely to start. There will be written policies, and procedures, and production records. There will be five people that will need to run computers.

There will be need for a network and IT resources. They may even need to be ISO certified, and hire me to set up their system, or be audited by me when they get their registrar lined up.

An administrative assistant will need to be hired. Work expands to fit the number of people.

Our heroes will be running a complex organization. This is the very thing they were trying to get away from. Does the excitement they got from creating and introducing some innovative product, or give some innovative service offset the headaches they now have?

This is the point at which they may feel the need to declare victory and walk away.

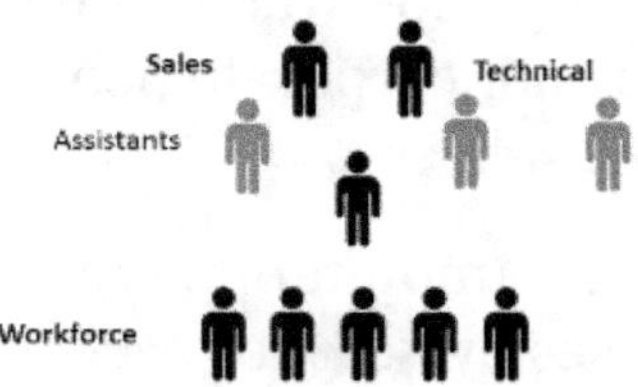

## Problem 9: Grow or Sell?

At this point, they may very well be able to live out the dream, and sell out to "the man." Very often this is some major corporation or competitor. The skills that the founders have, in their way, no longer fit the business. But, maybe by this time, and this much hard work, they may be willing to graduate. It depends on their age and temperament.

I've also seen it happen that the business gets bigger and better under their current management. New locations are started. There is expansion. But what has to happen is that the original founders have to recognize their own incompetence, and bring in professional managers that have their acts together. This also requires a different skillset, and our entrepreneurial founders may find themselves unsatisfied emotionally from this experience. "We can't hire good people" they say. What they mean is they can't find someone as passionate for the startup as they were, and they would be right.

You know what impresses me about Steve Jobs? He was bright enough to adapt to that reality. He was able to transform himself (barely, if you read the bios) and recognized that he needed to bring in the pros, but he then whined about their skill set and passion when he hired them. I have a link in the links and references on this topic.

Are our startup people going to be willing to do this? Maybe not. At which point, maybe there will be growing pains, and even worse (and I have seen this too) they will start to do a mediocre job. Product recalls will happen. They will get customer complaints because their supervisor, who was originally a low wage worker, can't possibly cope with corporate structure.

They will start to lose major customers. They'll be forced to do firefighting. They will lose operational control. Their "advantage" in the marketplace will be gone.

Some consultant will be brought in to "rescue them." You know where to find me.

You want to know what would be even worse? They could hire their kids.

## Steve Jobs

If you want to go back into ancient history: Apple Computer was founded in 1976 in a garage near San Francisco.

By 1985, the "professional managers" and angel investors made him mad enough to stomp out, and he went to his happy place. His skillset as an entrepreneur didn't fit his organization. By 1997 he swooped in, re-bought the company, and using his other skillset, namely being visionary, helped him bring the company back from the verge of bankruptcy.

It's an interesting story, but not everyone that rich would have come back.

Links and References

COME IN! WE'RE OPEN

# 09 The Family Business

We're now going to tackle the case of the family business. When I get around to it, there will be a very interesting novel focusing on this as a horror story, but for now, let's focus on the issue of a family business, and people not doing their jobs

## Why this is Important

According to one of the references I've posted in the links and references, something on the order of half of the nation's GDP is generated by businesses with two or more family members. However, 70% of family businesses never make it to the third generation, so there are obviously some issues with them doing their jobs.

The other reason this is important is if you are a non-family member getting into a family business situation, there are some challenges.

## Why People Don't Do Their Jobs: Family Business Version

These things start to fall into patterns after a while. Here's the table for the Family Business

| Reason | Description | Comments |
|---|---|---|
| 1 | Personality Issues | "Driver" and "Family" are often difficult people and have |

| | | |
|---|---|---|
| | | psychological issues |
| 2 | Lack of Processes | Processes are "whatever the boss says." Everybody has 4 bosses. Family issues are dragged into the workplace. Discipline is selectively enforced. No one dares say 'no." |
| 3 | Alarm systems are non-existent | Driver and Family are kept in a bubble. Low levels unable to communicate problems to management. Warning signs are ignored. |
| 4 | Employees are disengaged or ticked off | Driver can't come up with a reason for the existence of the business, other than for themselves. Kids are promoted over high-performing outsiders. |
| 5 | Denial and Dishonesty | Lack of control systems and discipline lead to ethical issues. Driver fails to spot external |

| | | |
|---|---|---|
| | | issues. |
| 6 | Technical limitations | Business is limited to the expertise of the "Driver." Lack of adoption of best industry practices and other outside influences. Lack of knowledge of regulations. |
| 7 | Managers are weak or nonexistent | Line managers have no authority. Driver and family make decisions. Employees learn to circumvent the system. |
| 8 | Resource Issues | Equipment and systems are not aggressively replaced. "Cheap" bosses don't want to spend money to maintain the business. |
| 9 | Entrenched Mediocrity | Mediocre managers and employees don't get fired. Ineffective processes and equipment are not |

| | | |
|---|---|---|
| | | upgraded. |

## The Driver

I'm going to start more or less where I left off regarding a business startup. Let's say, for example, there is a startup situation, and the boss is something called a "Driver."

The "Driver" personality type was identified as far back as Ancient Greece. I can't say it better than Lucas who describes these people as follows:

*Dominant, independent, candid, decisive, pragmatic, and efficient. This personality type emphasizes overcoming opposition to accomplish results. Driver personalities tend to focus on tasks, seek power and control, and need challenges.*

This is your "Driver" personality, who, through the force of his or her own will, starts a business and tries to make it work. Very often, this is a situation where there are two people in the initial startup, and one of them gets ticked off and/or loses interest and leaves.

Here's their first org chart:

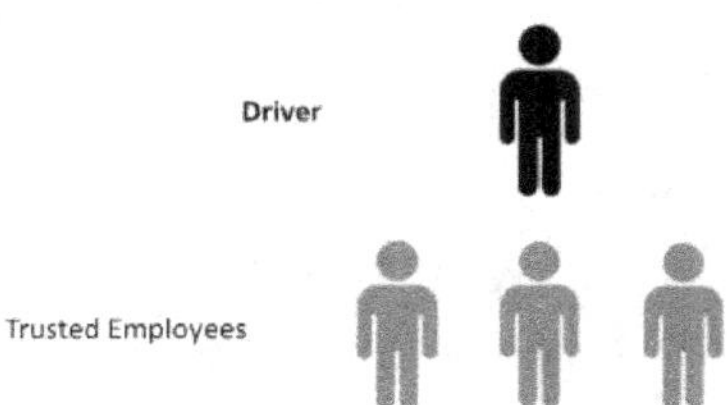


I have observed a few instances of this. The "Driver" realizes they can't do it alone, and hires a handful of Trusted Employees to work with/for them. These employees may keep the business running, and keep the "Driver" out of jail, because they provide the counterbalancing opposite to the Driver's personality. The opposite of the "Driver" is considered to be the "analytical" personality type, so to make a long story short, the most successful of these have the ability to tell the "Driver" "NO."

Drivers hate the word "No" but the best drivers understand that there are times they need to hear it, and keep these people around.

Your classic group of these might be an accountant, a technical person and an administrator. Drivers very often take the sales role themselves, because no one can self-promote a Driver like the Driver him or herself.

## How to know that the Boss is a "Driver" Personality?

He, and it is usually a "he", will tell you. Very often, his or her name is on the door.

Years ago, I was working as a technical person, and we had a customer down in Florida who was this type. He had a technical problem, like Drivers very often do, and I went in with the sales guy in response.

The place was at the end of a very long country road in among the trees. The road widened out into a clearing, and there was a collection of metal buildings, one of which was a church, paid for by the "Driver."

We got into this fellow's office and there was a stuffed bear in the lobby wearing one of those bucket hats that you don't now see very often.

A few minutes later, the boss appeared, wearing the same hat. This was in June, and the place was all decorated for "Father's Day" in that even the non-family employees embraced this fellow's role as the "father" of the business.

## The Next Stage of Development

Sometimes, the Driver is able to overcome barriers, which is what they do, and make the business a bit of a success. The "trusted employees" keep things on track, and it manages to expand.

I said earlier about the size of a business reaching a critical point when it gets to about 15 people. That goes double for this kind of business, because there is a limit to the number of people that "the driver" can boss around.

The trusted employees get to be some kind of buffer in the workplace against the excesses of the Driver. What that also means is that the trusted employees get to be a little co-dependent on "the Driver" since they also do the job of dealing with the driver's inner insecurities. It's hard to be one of those people, and the Driver is very often a little manipulative, and also, throws money at this layer generously because he or she realizes the value.

Does this occasionally become abusive? Well, that is in the eye of the beholder, but since we're writing the script, let's say it does.

In this type of organization, there are several failure modes, the number one of which is lack of processes and procedures. Everybody does what the Driver says. That is another thing that limits the growth of the business. Lack of consistent processes and procedures is a major factor in people not doing their jobs, because the procedures can change without notice.

Here's our new org chart:

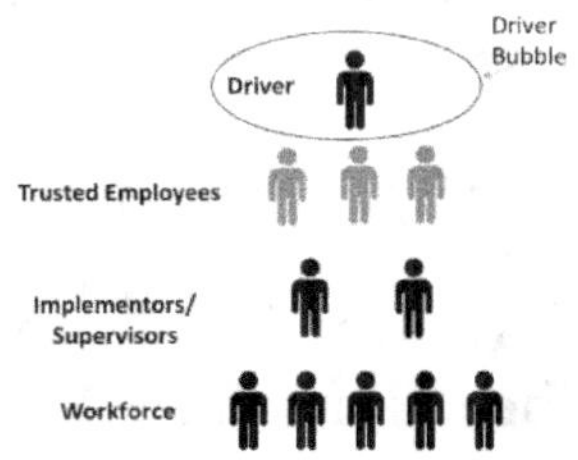

## Thought Questions

Let's look at this from the viewpoint of the lowest level employees. They may or may not report directly to a supervisor.

Do they have passion for the business? Well, once in a while you'll find a "Driver" that takes the time to be around the low-level employees and share this passion with them. But mainly, the Driver is focused on taking over the world. Therefore, the low-level employees are likely not to be tuned into the corporate mission, assuming there is one. The Driver may, in some cases, actually resent their presence.

Are they going to listen to their supervisors? No. they also see that the real authority in the business is the Driver and the Trusted Employees, and they are not likely to respect the line managers, and that weakens the line managers' ability to actually develop and enforce policies that keep people doing their jobs.

So not only are the low-level employees disengaged, and ignore their processes, if they have any to begin with, they're disconnected from the underlying rationale for the business.

From the point of view of the front-line supervisors. Do you like your job? Of course, you don't. You have to be responsible for the behavior of the low-level employees, who can go over your head if need be. You have to implement the processes and procedures of the Driver, which often are not especially well communicated or thought out. You may have resource limitations.

## Process Measurements are Missing

You may also lack an objective measurement of success. We will talk about this a bit later. It's useful for the business to have metrics of one kind or another so that the employees and supervisor know whether or not they're doing their jobs, but in one of these businesses, these systems are weak. The business is running, or not running, according to the reality of the Driver, which is very often not objective.

You might have the best production day ever, and be proud of your workforce, and have the Driver come down to the plant floor and give you hell because of something else that was going on in his or her life.

From the point of view of the "Trusted Employees." Do you like your job? We also know that one or more of you have to play psychologist occasionally to soothe the Driver, who may lack the ability to self-soothe. You may even see your job as keeping the boss in a bubble so that he or she doesn't fly off the handle.

You also know that there's no such thing as a promotion, and also, you do a lot of work that wouldn't be tolerated in a "normal" corporate environment. You may also form sort of a trauma-bond with the Driver, whose qualities you sometimes admire.

Very often, unfortunately, this evolves into sort of an emotional and physical attachment, and if that happens, the whole business could spin out of control. That also has a de-motivating effect on the layers of the business around them, and can be a drain on the Driver's productivity, if you're catching my drift.

We touched on this earlier to the extent that it is easy for this layer of employee to actually take advantage of the situation, and not do their jobs. The "Employee" having a special relationship with their boss and being immune from firing is a strong de-motivator for all of the levels of the business, and may lead to other employees not doing their jobs.

## Communication Issues and the "Driver Bubble"

Here's the most dangerous aspect about any of this. The Trusted Employees may keep the manager in an "information bubble." If the alarm systems and other metrics in the business aren't objective, there is a real danger that the Trusted Employees may become "trained" to keeping the managers in the dark.

In the innocent case, the Trusted Employees learn what will and won't set off the Driver's temper, if he or she has one, and act accordingly.

In the non-innocent case, the Trusted Employees could easily move to the dark side, and start to exploit their personal situation by corruption of one kind or another. Embezzlement from a family business is common enough.

The information bubble can easily work the other way, where the Driver will hide bad news from the rest of the organization, and no one wants that either. That keeps lower-level employees in the dark, and has potential to tick them off. Who wants to hear through the back door that the company has lost its biggest customer and half of them are going to be laid off? People need information.

## Can the Driver Prevent Any of This?

Sure. The Driver can set up systems and processes in their business, and maintain the discipline of the business in dealing with the Trusted Employees and everybody else.

The Driver may back up employees who follow the structure, and discourage end-runs around them. This is particularly important in the case of quality control procedures, which are set up to keep crap from getting to the customers.

The Driver may insist on a strict code of ethical behavior to keep funny business from happening. He or she may have systems to verify whether the accounting system is functioning properly. The Driver may be customer focused, and have a corporate mission, which is clearly communicated in the business. That would direct all levels of the organization to do their jobs. He or she may bring in outside resources occasionally to help him or her do this.

The Driver may also have the open-mindedness to listen to suggestions from employees, and also, apply resources to the business if needed. He or she may, despite temptation, be patient and willing to accept bad news from the organization and be committed to making it better for everybody.

He or she may reward performance, and encourage innovative thinking among the crew, who he or she may take time to understand personally.

Or not. Depends on the Driver.

There is an article presented in the Links and References that describes the various reasons that a business doesn't scale up, and as we said earlier, the business starts to be limited by the Driver.

## Enter the Family

The "Driver" business model is already fragile.

Let's write the following script: The Driver gets to be about 60, and there are some 30-year-old adult children around who need jobs, and the kids are brought in to run the business. From the point of view of the Driver, this is a good thing, because he or she may want to pass the business down to them and pass on the pride in having built some lasting enterprise that makes customers happy.

It doesn't have to be kids. It can be nieces and nephews, or brothers or cousins or other people that have some relationship with the boss.

Since we are writing the script, let's say that it's the kids. There's your first clue. In the eyes of the Driver, they're still kids. The second clue is that they need jobs. They haven't managed to be self-supporting.

Here are some potential failure modes that will cause people not to do their jobs.

| Issue | Description | Comments |
| --- | --- | --- |
| 1 | Kids lack the personal qualities needed for leadership | Regression toward the mean (Genetics). |
| 2 | Kids aren't experienced in business, and haven't been "steeled." | Lack of appreciation for the hard work it took to establish the business and its systems. |
| 3 | Kids are weak | Kids had to put up with the Driver all of their lives, which is often difficult. (C-PTSD) |
| 4 | Kids are entitled | Kids lack the benefit of actually having personal achievements. |
| 5 | Kids don't respect the processes and systems | Kids disrespect the chain of command, don't pay attention to processes and policies. |
| 6 | Kids disengaged from the mission | To the extent that there is one, kids don't appreciate |

| | | |
|---|---|---|
| | and/or customers | the customer. |
| 7 | Kids actually resent the business | The business often represents time spent away from them as "children." |
| 8 | Kids are terrible leaders themselves | Kids manage to tick off or discourage everybody else in the business, particularly the Trusted Employees. |
| 9 | Kids provide an additional information bubble | Kids hide bad news, and cut off the trusted employees from information sharing. |

Here's our new organizational chart:

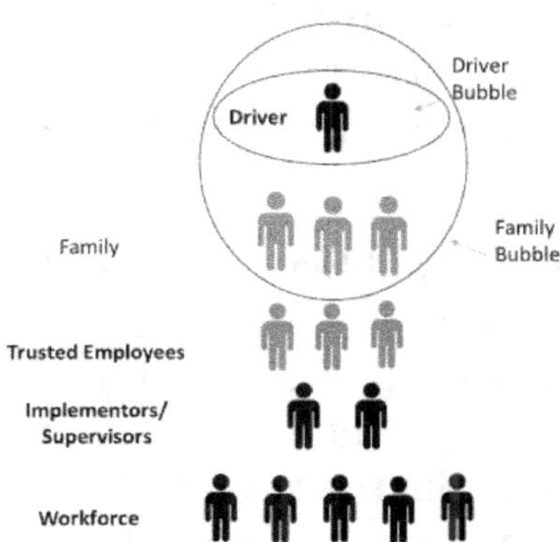


## Effects on Workplace Culture

I have seen cases where this has worked. The family members start at a low enough level in the business so that the line employees and the trusted employees develop respect for their work ethic and other personal qualities.

But I have seen plenty of cases where the opposite happens, with potentially disastrous results. Regular employees, who are disengaged, also become resentful and distrusting, and they won't do their jobs.

This is particularly important in the area of quality control, where if quality control procedures and systems are short-circuited, the rest of the employees will question the fundamental commitment of the business to the marketplace.

This is also important in businesses where there has been a supportive company culture previously, but the kids just don't get it, and blow the whole thing up.

## Effects on Communications

However isolated the Driver was in the original case, it gets even worse in the case where a family layer is installed in the business.

Now, there is a second bubble: A "Driver Bubble" and a "Family Bubble" where even the trusted employees are cut off from the boss. These trusted employees who understand "the mission" now have diminished ability to point problems out from the Driver, including ethical and legal problems, and there is a chance that the integrity of the business itself is in issue.

Further communications issues can result if the family members don't communicate among themselves. This is very problematic for the people at the low levels of the business who now have four bosses, and they are not in agreement on policy and functional processes.

The normal business hierarchy is disrupted, trusted employees become disengaged, and there is enhanced risk.

## One Last Scenario

Since we're writing the script on this: What happens when the Driver suddenly departs?

Here's our new org chart:

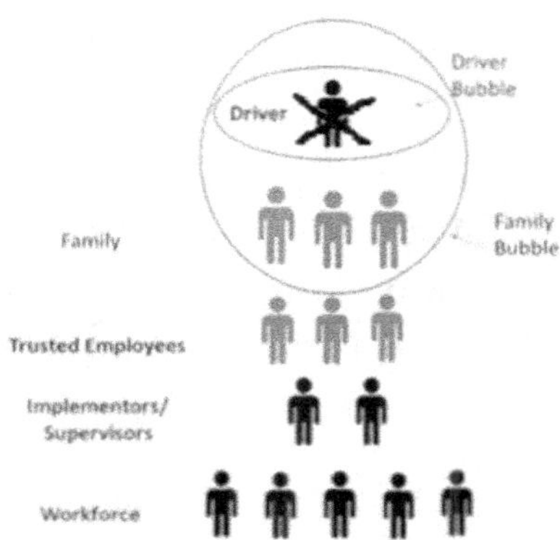


Now what? First of all, since the business was being held together by the will of the Driver, there is risk that the whole thing will end up shutting down. The more likely scenario is that the business will be sold, with the resulting effects on employee morale.

Unless there are clear rules of authority and responsibility that are respected by the Family layer there is sure to be jealousy, infighting, and potential for mischief.

The Trusted Employees, who are codependent on the Driver emotionally and from an employment standpoint are now lost, and whatever resentment there may have already been from the kids being brought in now goes through the roof, they also don't do their jobs.

The only guard rails on the kids' behavior, namely the force of the Driver is now gone, but they very often lack the wisdom and experience of the Driver. The results of that could be a disaster. However bad it was in the first place the communications issues may now be amplified.

Whatever discipline and respect for the processes of the business that there were in the first place are potentially going to be weaker.

There are serious legal issues. In a sole proprietorship, if the owner dies, the business immediately dissolves. If there is lack of clear succession planning, there could be chaos. Customers won't get their products, and people won't do their jobs.

## It's Not Hopeless

Sorry for being a downer on this. Like all reasons that people don't do their jobs, there is a range of outcomes. Some of these family businesses become huge and famous. The Lego Company and the Henkel Corporation are two examples that survived the founders, have disciplined systems and beloved products, and that is fine.

They eventually become professionally run businesses.

The Ford Motor Company, whatever else you say, falls into that category too. They evolved from the concept of the Driver to become professionally managed and self-sustaining. The fourth generation is now running the Detroit Lions, who have success every few decades. It was acquired by the Ford family in 1961 with humorous results.

If you want to see a funny movie about this topic, I have linked the trailer to the film "Tommy Boy" (Paramount 1995)

Tommy Boy

https://youtu.be/9btKFrFhq28?si=-ooL5RxfGBSWY5Io

If you want to see a "less funny" movie about this topic, all I would do is direct you to any of the films about the British monarchy. That family business has been going on for centuries, with drama, subversion, employee disengagement, murder, mayhem, scandal, and everything else. People do what they do, until they can't.

PS: The family business that had the bear in the lobby still exists, and has outlived the owner, and the website has on it a salute and bio of the founder and owner, minus the bucket hat.

In this case, one of the younger sons seems to have been competent enough to eventually take the place over. He would be about 70 now, for what that is worth, and has probably earned it.

We knew him as a fairly grease-covered plant floor supervisor. I won't tell you who it is, out of respect for the confidentiality of the business, but will disclose the website if you contact me.

There is a funny story about me not doing my job with regards to this, which also had a humorous element.

Links and References

# 10 Raising the Red Flag

We're going to talk some more about alarm systems now. As we're about to see, there are a lot of different kinds of alarms, and they all have one thing in common. They're used to alert some human about some undesirable condition.

What the human then does in response is the key issue.

As the alarm system increases in complexity, the number of humans that can understand and react to the condition will decrease.

All of this is critical to people doing, or not doing, their jobs.

https://youtu.be/M2xhj9D9Zxg

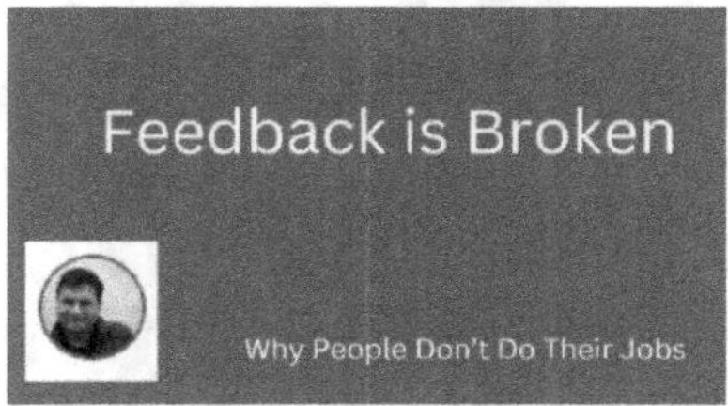

Feedback is Broken
Why People Don't Do Their Jobs

## Alarm Negativity

Part of why this is an important is that an alarm usually flies in the face of "positive reinforcement." We talked about that in the chapter on Operant Conditioning in my first book.

Positive reinforcement is considered better, but in the case of alarms it is impractical. For example, I am in a room right now which has a smoke alarm. Its job is to give a loud, unpleasant noise if there is smoke, and my job, if I hear it, is to take some kind of action.

Most often it is to remove whatever I've just burned off of the stovetop.

But, taking the other point of view, the alarm could, if we wanted it to, give a positive message. A little voice could say "Congratulations Jim, your room doesn't have any smoke in it at the moment." The result of that is that we silly humans, with limited bandwidth, would tune it out.

So that's one of the fundamental flaws of alarms. The whole idea of an alarm is negative and people tune it out if it sounds too often.

https://youtu.be/B68AlS3PpWI

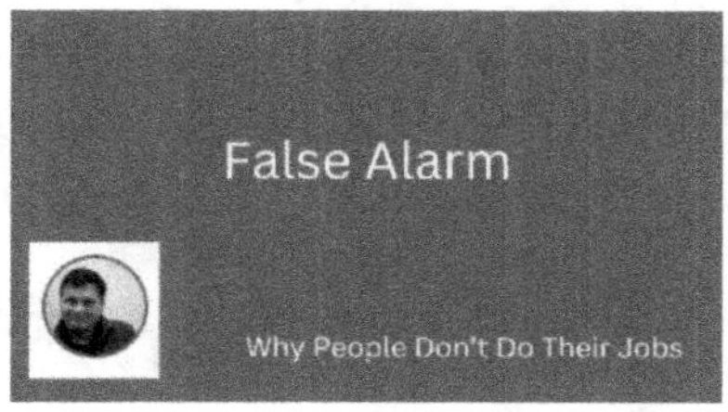


## Alarm Basics

Here's a two-dimensional matrix. Nobody thinks about this stuff fundamentally.

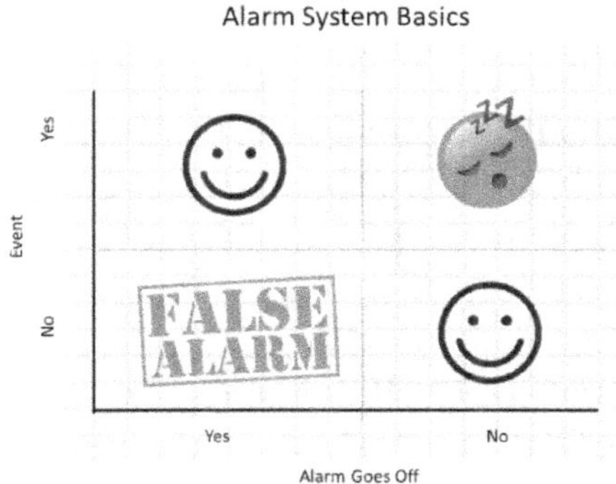


Let's just say, to make it complicated, that this is a big industrial metal detector in a place that makes paper products of some type. Paperboard manufacture, for example, is one place where this might be used.

As part of this process there is something called "tramp metal" which is little pieces of metal that get into the material. It is particularly bad toward the end of the process. The paper people really hate this because little pieces of metal that are embedded in trees really mess up their processing equipment.

In either one of these cases industrial metal detectors are used to screen this stuff out before it does serious damage.

In a case like this, there are four possible situations. The good condition, namely a little piece of metal being in the material stream, doesn't happen. That's a good thing, because we don't want it to happen. So, we're down on the lower right side of the graph, with the smiley face.

In the lower left is a condition called the false alarm. This situation happens so often in car alarms that 97% of the time they are ignored. In this case, the condition doesn't happen, namely there is no metal, and the alarm goes off anyway.

In the industrial situation you don't want that because you don't want people to jump through a lot of hoops to fix some issue that didn't happen. After a while, they just ignore the alarm.

## Sleeping Through Your Alarm

The upper right is annoying, when the alarm goes off properly, but the employee doesn't react. In the industrial experience it is dangerous and expensive. It's where a piece of metal gets past the metal detector without the alarm sounding, and it has a chance to screw something up.

To avoid this, you need to test the metal detector sometimes. There is a controlled piece of metal that is run through the gadget just to make sure it works. One possible failure on this is that the crew is too lazy to test the metal detector, with potentially serious results. I have seen several of these that are "working fine" until I insisted that the crew test it like they should have.

So, this can be relatively harmless or very serious and expensive. Some huge, smooth embossing roller could get a ding in it, and mess up a lot of beautiful finished product.

In the upper left is the situation you want. The event happens and the alarm goes off. Your crew can then (hopefully) take action.

## The Alarm Reaction

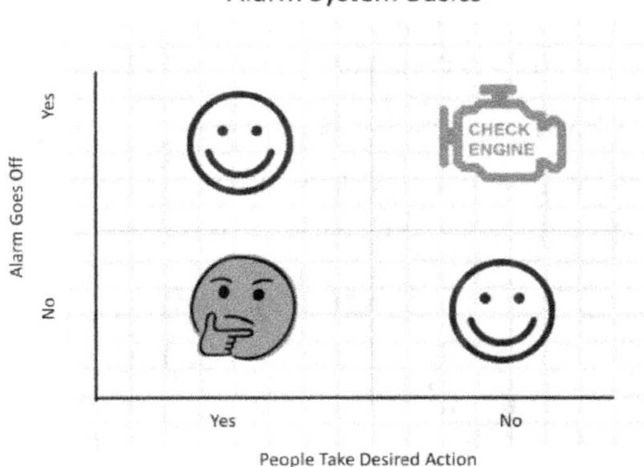


Well, normally when the alarm is installed in the first place, some thought is given to this question. The employees that operate this equipment are trained to investigate and contain the situation. And, in theory, when new employees are hired, they're brought in on the protocol through some kind of training.

In that case, you're in the upper left. The alarm sounds, people take action, they shut down the equipment and find the piece of metal, and everything is fine.

The upper right is a case where the alarm goes off and people either ignore it, or kind of shrug it off. I have a junky Nissan where this happens if you don't screw the gas cap down properly. The car functions fine, but the light comes on, and I shrug and keep driving. For all I know, the sensor itself can be malfunctioning.

But, in the industrial situation that's terrible because there is some potentially dangerous condition. This is particularly dangerous if it has been a long time since the alarm went off. Several generations of employees and supervisors could have come and gone since the last alarm.

An example of how you can avoid alarm indifference is have drills. This is your fire drill situation, where you train people to react in some way if the fire alarm goes off.

I guess it's fairly obvious that you want to live mostly in the lower right. The alarm doesn't go off, and people don't react. Business as usual, as long as you're sure the alarm is working properly.

## The Lower Left

This is a case where the alarm doesn't go off, and the employees take action anyway. Let's say, in the case of our metal detector, that the action is to take the equipment down, and clean it out proactively. This might be some kind of preventive maintenance operation that keeps the event from happening in the first place.

The only problem with this is that there is a cost associated with it. You don't want your employees shutting the equipment down because you lose time and money.

Plus, if the job is particularly annoying, such as cleaning out a sewer pipe, the employees will resist it.

## Alarm System Failure Modes

I actually asked AI about the solution to this sticky problem, and got the very common answer "it depends."

The food industry people are really sensitive to this sort of thing because they have to process some sort of natural material, which very often is handled through primitive augers and conveyor systems (I am thinking "corn" here) and then process it with 100% certainty and deliver it to the consumers as pure as driven snow, or purer if possible.

There is an interesting forum that I have posted in the links and references about this topic, as it applies to metal detectors, but the same is true for detecting any kind of hazard.

Any system that you develop and install is highly dependent on cost. Let's say hypothetically that the more expensive system the better, which is usually the way life works. How much money are you willing to spend to have one piece of metal per year escape detection. If the cost of the metal detector exceeds the cost of the failure, as measured somehow, that is the definition of overkill.

I would love to find actual data on this topic, but this information is very specific to the type of alarm, the importance of the event, and so on. It becomes a business decision.

## Alarm System Failure Modes

Here are some alarm system failure modes, roughly in decreasing order of their frequency.

| Frequency | Description |
|---|---|
| 1 | Fake Alarm (See Below) |
| 2 | False Alarm |
| 3 | Alarm works and people have no idea what to do |
| 4 | Alarm goes off, correctly, and people ignore it |
| 5 | Alarm quits working and people are happy (no protocol to test the alarm) |
| 6 | Alarm functions properly but people go to some effort to shut it up |
| 7 | Alarm was installed properly originally, but process changes happen to make it less effective |
| 8 | Alarm system inadequately designed or improperly installed to begin with |

| | |
|---|---|
| 9 | People deliberately don't sound an alarm to avoid 3, 4 and 5 above |
| 10 | A condition occurs that you don't have an alarm for |

## Fake and/or Nuisance Alarms

As I said above, there are all sorts of alarms, one of which is the "alert" that shows up in your email that says your account has been shut off, or your package is late, or someone has hacked your account. If you'd just send a few hundred dollars to someone they will fix it for you.

I have about 10 spam calls a day that say:" Your SAM registration is about to expire." That's so they can sell me the service of resetting it for me.

What that makes me want to do is ignore all alerts, including some that might be legitimate.

I am ready to say that this is the most common type of alarm right now as I write this. Whoever in the universe is in charge of controlling this activity is not doing their job.

## Guard Dogs

Speaking of alarms, humans have used guard dogs for many centuries to warn them that some coyote is about to steal their sheep. Prior to that, the dogs were trained to bark if a saber-toothed cat was about to bite their master's head off.

Some dogs were bred for this expressed purpose.

This is an example of an alarm system that was installed in the first place under one set of conditions, but conditions have changed. Most of us no longer live in a world where our sheep are in jeopardy, and our caves are being attacked by saber toothed cats.

But the dogs still have this ability, and don't hesitate to bark all night if something is bothering them. The neighbors complain and call animal control if that is the case. This is an example of (6) above where the alarm functions properly, but people deliberately try to shut it up.

## Babies

Babies are people that are underdeveloped physically but are intellectually normal.

Their "alarm" is to cry, if some condition develops that they don't like.

Their caregivers are "trained" to respond to them in various ways. Their main caregiver, who is usually "mom" is typically the best at understanding the alarm, depending on the time of day and tone, and goes through troubleshooting to shut it off. Feed. Change Diaper. Burp. Play with.

A less trained individual (Dad or Babysitter) may have a lot more difficulty understanding and reacting to the alarm when it is sounded.

I believe that tonally, the alarms in manufacturing that most closely mimic this have been found to be the most effective.

## Alarm Stories

I have a few examples that have been in the news lately, and they are all related to this topic. This is typical of the year 2024 but these examples have been repeated over and over throughout history.

In the case of the East Palestine railroad disaster, a train carrying a couple of dozen tanker cars of hazardous materials derailed and released a huge cloud of toxic fumes over the town. This is still under investigation, but the preliminary finding is that the detectors that the railroad installed to warn the crew that a car was on fire either malfunctioned or was ignored by the inexperienced crew, resulting in disaster. That would be either #3 or #4 above.

In the case of the Rensselaer Laboratory fail, a freezer containing a 20-year-old cancer experiment stopped working, and an alarm sounded. Through a series of unfortunate events, a subcontractor unplugged the freezer to shut up the alarm, causing the loss of a million-dollar piece of valuable research. This would fall under Type 3 above, where the training systems didn't extend to subcontractors, and also #6 where the subcontractor just shut it up.

In the case of the Lahaina, Hawaii, wildfire disaster a fire alarm consisting of 80 sirens was not sounded, in the face of a raging wild fire. The resulting fire burned down the entire town, causing untold damage and loss of life. Preliminary investigations say that is a case of Class 9 above, where some decision is made not to sound an alarm because it might upset people.

In the case where a chocolate factory in Pennsylvania blew up, evidence has revealed that the employees smelled gas for a few days before the explosion. The stink in natural gas, by the way is deliberately added so that people know that it is leaking, thus making it a form of alarm. The question is, was the alarm ignored (4 above) or was the alarm raised, but not acted on (3 above). The investigation and lawsuits are still underway.

I have links in the links and references on this, for your further entertainment. We can play this game from now on when something stupid happens, and people don't do their jobs because an ineffectively managed alarm system.

## Alarm Story, 20th Century

In the place I worked a few years ago, there was a big mixer, and loading this thing, by hand, were a couple of laborers. A supervisor was in charge of actually operating the mixer. The laborers were cutting the material that they were weighing, and loading a big scale, which was monitored by a control system, which in those days was pre-digital. The material was hard, and difficult to cut, with one of those big guillotine cutters.

Here is a photo, except in that era, there was no safety guard on the front.

If the weigh belt personnel got the weight wrong a little red light went on. It forced the operators to take weight off the belt, or to add weight in order for the weight to be right. The batch wouldn't charge until they got it right.

There was a button below the red light which was the manual override. If the operator felt like being a nice guy, he could hit the button and the batch would charge into the mixer. If the operators took too long to adjust the weight, the whole process would lose efficiency. Everybody was measured on the number of batches mixed. If I am not mistaken, the workers got piece work rate, which meant that the more batches were mixed, the higher the pay. This was about 600 pounds of material, being weighed every 3 minutes or so. Hard work for anybody.

As it turned out, the operator felt like being a really nice guy. He had a set of jumper wires, and he permanently hotwired the override button so that even if the light went on, which it did, the weighers weren't required to get the weight right.

As it also turned out this particular supervisor had a lot of outside interests since he was running the bar across the street from the plant during the day. Double dipping on a job was fairly common in that era. He had his stuff.

Eventually someone figured out what was happening and they fired him. He probably wasn't all that sad but missed the generous benefit package.

The failure mode was number 6 above, the alarm functioned correctly but the supervisor shut it up. I also have to say that the process metric, namely throughput, was probably not well thought out from a management standpoint.

They may have been better off getting the weighments correct, and that is another potential failure mode. Having a system measurement that measures the wrong thing is not good either. I guess you would call that a potential failure mode 8, the "throughput" metric was improperly designed and encouraged people to cut corners.

Links and References

# 11 Why Your Space Shuttle Blew Up

In our journey through human failure, and preventable disasters, we're now going to focus on a few specific examples. We're going to start with the topic of why your space shuttle blew up.

Before we get too far into it, we're going to have to have a conversation about standard operating procedures, which we call SOP.

There are a lot of other names for this, including "Standard Practice", "Standard Protocol", "Work Instructions", "Standard Work" and a lot of others. In the medical industry, this may be called the "Device History Record." Each organization has a name for it. At the famous Swedish furniture store, it's called the "instruction manual."

How about this? Rituals. Customs. Rites. There is a religious element to some of this.

https://youtu.be/71v1cj0Yssg

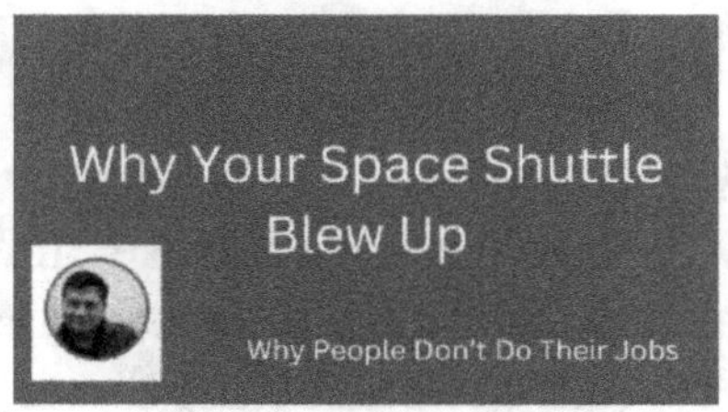


## Standard Operating Procedures

Reviewing standard operating procedures is part of my job, and I actually look at a dozen or more every time I work. That makes well over 6000 of these, in all sorts of different types of operations. They come in basically two types: Screwed up, and basically okay.

Standard operating procedures, in their purest form, are a method of communication. They are a message to the future. They are a description of the methods the workers used to produce, or assemble, or mix, or administer whatever it is they're working on.

The first Standard Operating Procedure in history is titled "How to Capture a Bison" and it was painted on the inside of a cave, somewhere between 20,000 and 50,000 years ago, in Lascaux, France.

Standard Operating Procedures, like other forms of human writing, were produced because there are limits to the memory of a single person.

In any complex operation, as Betty Crocker would tell you, there is only so much that any worker can remember. It's a way to capture the "right way" to do anything.

The methods and procedures used for running a business are an essential part of an organization's value. I once worked on a startup project someplace that was exotic. The organization did what we talked about earlier: bulldozed a section of jungle, constructed a little factory, hired a workforce, and had nothing. It was not until the Standard Operating Procedure was captured that it became a little business.

## Operating Procedures: The British Standard

The British Navy advanced this idea to the maximum level possible. As they were conquering the world in the 17th through 19th Century, it came to their attention that it would improve efficiency if everything in their organization was standardized. That includes building materials and methods, especially ship operation and methods. There were any number of regulations for doing anything.

That way, if someone was transferred from ship to ship, they didn't need to learn a lot of new operating procedures. They could more or less rely on the British Standard to maintain basic continuity.

What that did, however, was advance to a high level a form of employee called a "paper pusher" because a huge bureaucracy had to be developed to capture, maintain, and change these standards in a known way, and then communicate the changes to all of the remote operations.

And there had to be an archive of some type so that someone in 1888 could refer back to what the standard was in 1866 to understand how things were put together.

My favorite story on this is the train station in Kuala Lumpur that is built to withstand 12 inches of snow, courtesy of being constructed using the British Standard.

It was a history book, in a way, that captured how things were done in the past.

## Written vs. Oral Standard Operating Procedures

In simple organizations, it is common enough for the "Standard Operating Procedures" to be verbal rather than written. That is still fine except for two things: No one lives forever, and in this day and age, there is rapid turnover, so it is quite possible for somebody to leave the organization and take a lot of the knowledge with them.

There are standard operating procedures that are part of the basic training in certain activities. For example, in Nursing, there are certain jobs, such as taking blood pressure and drawing blood that are standardized within that industry. That enables the workforce to take certain skills from place to place as well, so that if an organization hires a nurse, or a plumber or welder, for that matter, there is a basic set of skills that person has that is standardized on an industry wide basis.

This also works for non-human-invasive activities like being a server in a restaurant. There are variations from one organization to another regarding greeting the customers, taking orders and submitting them to the kitchen, doing customer relations, and others. This varies slightly from place to place, but in some of the big organizations, like the giant chain restaurants, this is also standardized as part of the marketing and product identity.

Here's a very famous example from the movie "Office Space" which I like a lot.

## Joanna Doesn't Have Enough "Flair"

https://www.youtube.com/watch?v=F7SNEdjftno

In this scene, Joanna is caught wearing "only" fifteen pieces of "Flair". This scene brilliantly pointed out the idea that once a procedure is established, there are two kinds of people, those who are following it and those who are not.

What that also means is that as an organization, you need to think through what happens to an employee that follows the procedure to the letter and no more, or refuses to follow the procedure, and when it becomes a fireable offense.

On the basis of this scene, the TGI Friday's Corporation reportedly eliminated the requirement for wearing "flair" because they finally realized the silliness of the whole thing. My further guess is that sarcastic customers were teasing the wait people about having too little or too much.

In the dynamite factory, the employees all need to be certified dynamite handlers. This activity is considered important enough that it is a federal requirement, and is taken very seriously, at least in that place. I have a link that describes the process of getting an explosive handling permit. In addition to the filling out of forms, a prospective explosives handler needs to be interviewed and examined regarding the handling of explosives prior to doing so. Does that mean that there are no people in the US who carelessly handle dynamite? No, I am sure there are plenty of idiots that violate the Dynamite SOP, but at least some effort has been made to limit the repercussions to as few people as possible.

## Inane and Stupid Standard Operating Procedures

I guess that does bring up the question of how a Standard Operating Procedure is developed.

The best kind of operating procedure is one where the essential task is made more efficient, and not made stupid. Who is the judge of that? There may be differences of opinion.

What normally happens in a place is that a procedure is developed on how to develop procedures. Ideally this procedure is developed by a person who is knowledgeable. In some places that is called a "subject matter expert." A determination is made whether the procedure should be a "requirement" or "suggestion." At some point there is also some controlled way to both ensure compliance and change it if needed.

Very often, in huge, complex organizations, there are huge books of these, or nowadays, a huge computer database of these, with a significant investment in human energy and money tied up in them.

And, there are third party auditors, like me, that have the gift of going into these places, actually reading the operating procedures, and figuring out whether the employees are still doing them. One of the weak links in this whole story is the idea that someone finds a better way to do something, takes a shortcut, and then doesn't report back to the authority people that the change was made.

This is one of the many places that the "Amorphous They" re-enter the scene. "They" are in some ivory tower, someplace, making rules that the employees on some dark, dirty factory floor somewhere need to follow, and "They" are very often limited in their knowledge of actual work conditions.

"They" might be an engineer, or some other person right out of college, or "they" might be an old-timer that hasn't been out on the floor for many years. I have stories on this. "They" might very well be someplace in some outside nation, who speaks one language, and the employees may be in the basement of a huge manufacturing plant somewhere in Iowa. You can see the drawbacks.

Why People Still Don't Do Their Jobs

https://youtu.be/XOHw49BHnsA

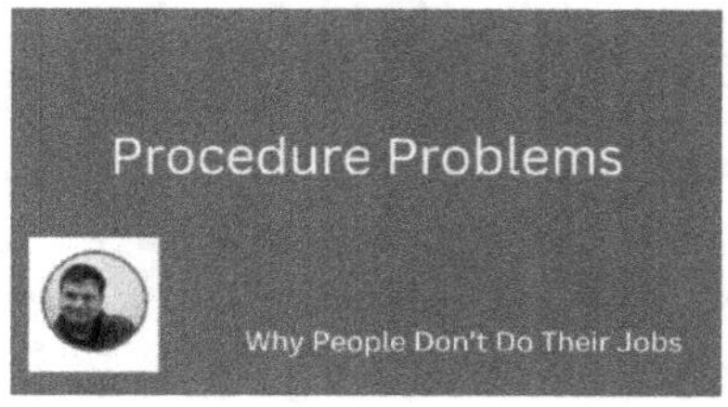


## Being Told What to Do

We've touched on this at several points. The Standard Operating Procedure is essentially regarded by some people as being told what to do, because it is.

Does anyone like being told what to do? Well, there are certain people that appreciate it for a while, when they are first introduced to a job. But as they become more experienced, and the job becomes more routine, do they still like being told what to do? Not necessarily. If you assemble one piece of Swedish furniture, you need the instructions. But, after the 500th of those same pieces of furniture, an ambitious employee will begin to second guess the instructions, and find better ways to do things. So, there may be some drift from the original standard operating procedure.

A less ambitious employee will just put the furniture together as directed. We may talk about "decaying compliance" at a later time.

Do you know who really hates following the operating procedures? Top Gun Pilots. We talked about them at length in my previous work, "Why People Don't Do Their Jobs." These people think they are better and smarter than the rule makers, because they are.

## Why Your Space Shuttle Blew Up

So now that you have the background on Standard Operating Procedures, let's think about this: Imagine the most complex vehicle ever invented by human civilization, with well over a million components, and countless operating procedures for doing anything. And imagine that same process being operated and managed literally by Top Gun Pilots.

Do you see the fundamental risk?

In retrospect it was inevitable.

On February 1, 2003, the space shuttle "Columbia" broke up as it re-entered the atmosphere, tragically killing the crew of seven astronauts, and distributing a carpet of debris for several hundred miles over Texas.

I will let you read some of the accounts of this in the linked article.

I have also linked a 264-page reference manual about various aspects of the Space Shuttle operations, that was prepared as part of the research on this complicated vehicle.

I have also linked the 399-page "Flight and Ground System Specification Book 1."

## The Investigation

This tragic incident precipitated a big investigation, which discovered the following:

The crash itself was caused by a large piece of foam insulation that fell off the solid rocket boosters during liftoff. This was despite the standard operating procedure which says the following:

*"Space Shuttle System, including the ground systems, shall be designed to preclude the shedding of ice and/or other debris from the Shuttle elements during pre-launch and flight operations that would jeopardize the flight crew, vehicle, mission success, or would adversely impact turnaround operations."*

*"No debris shall emanate from the critical zone of the External Tank on the launch pad or during ascent except for such material which may result from normal thermal protection system recession due to ascent heating."*

*Ground System Specification Book – Shuttle Design Requirements*

*CAIB Report, Vol. 1, p. 122*

Further investigation revealed that this particular condition had not only occurred on this flight, but on every other flight, an average of 142 times per flight.

So, this was a known condition that was allowed to continue despite obvious risk. This is one of the very definitions of Entrenched Mediocrity, which we talked about earlier.

The further question was asked, this being the case, why this happened? Why did the launch director and other personnel not shut the project down and fix the problem?

## The NASA Culture

There was a lot of finger-pointing, and this was mainly toward the launch director, whose job it should have been to shut the whole thing down and fix it.

But at the time, there was a lot of political resistance to telling the truth and shutting the project down.

Ultimately this was all blamed on the "NASA Culture" which is as follows:

*Nothing bad happened in the previous 112 flights, so therefore it must have been okay. This is what is known as "normalized deviance."*

*No one was allowed to speak up*

*No one had the authority to pull the plug*

*There was a bypass of the normal chain of command*

*The resultant investigations were quashed.*

On the basis of all of this, all was declared to be well, and the investigation, headed by a very experienced Naval officer who was not a Top Gun Pilot, made some recommendations. This included increased photography of the takeoffs to determine whether the vehicle was damaged, and instituting a backup plan to go up and rescue the crew if the same thing ever happened again.

The final flight of the program was in 2011, in total there were only 20 or so flights after the disaster.

No one was ever fired, no one went to jail, and the world seems to have moved on, except to say the idea of a "shuttle type" reusable launch vehicle seems to have died down a bit.

## What Is Happening Now

Well, it looks like NASA fulfilled its main mission, which was to make space travel so routine that people have stopped paying attention to it.

There are a variety of other nations and private organizations that have attempted space shots, and the launching of the James Webb Telescope has proven to be an extreme success. Like air travel once was, this has become a bit of a hobby for rich people.

There is such a thing as the "Artemis Project" which will launch a man and woman to the moon for some reason in 2024, and I have linked something called the IV&V facility which is doing a lot of work to make space travel safer.

I will be happy to have a discussion about this except to say that if any of these entities and organizations set up a lot of rules, and decide not to follow them, there will be more disasters. It's endemic in the human condition.

## General Words about Operating Procedures

In a general way, here is my accumulated wisdom on this, after having seen thousands of these things:

In the early stages of an organizational development, such as a startup, they're irrelevant. The hard headed technical people, like we talked about earlier, already know everything. The problems start to happen when they need to give their knowledge to others. In order to scale up, even if that only means adding a second shift, there needs to be some formalization of standard operating procedures, and resultant consequences for anybody who ignores them.

This often gets to the point where the founders of the business, who were stifled in their soul-crushing corporate jobs, start to hate it. They learn to short-circuit their own procedures.

The franchise outfits are experts at this ref: the "Flair" which are part of the standardization and marketing. The famous soft drinks that we produce in the USA taste exactly the same in Kuala Lumpur because of this standardization.

The next threshold is when an organization gets big and complex enough to hire humans to produce and manage the standard operating procedure documentation. These people had better be intimate in the process themselves or it causes a lot of problems. It further causes a lot of problems if there is no feedback system to change them and keep them updated. This is the emergence of the "Amorphous They" and resulting chaos. This is also where I, the third-party auditor, is sometimes hired to check up on the system.

Very often, this is the point at which the business, if successful, is sold to "the man" that is some professionally run organization who can't possibly have developed the innovation internally, and the original founders take the money and run. The standard operating procedures have to be formalized, if they have not been, in order to integrate into the parent company.

It is correct that an organization can get big and complex enough that operational consistency is more important than innovation. By this time, the Top Gun Pilots are weeded out of the organization, and go wherever they go. Standard Operating Procedures are declared to be sacrosanct and dogma. People are considered not to have done their jobs if they ignore the SOP. There is a whole little kabuki dance around the practice of detection and enforcement, like there is for speeding in your car.

At some point, the business becomes vulnerable to external dislocation. There may be technical innovation in their industry that causes the conventional wisdom to be out the window.

At the same time, they've weeded out all of their Top Gun Pilots and Technical Innovators, and they have a hell of a problem. They may do what I referred to in (6) above, which is buy some small, more agile competitor who has already solved the technical problems. The oilfield companies are brilliant at this. They allow wildcatters to go out and find oil, the unsuccessful ones starve out, and they buy the successful ones.

Anyway, your space shuttle blew up because of the following:

*Top gun pilots ignored the SOP.*

*There was too much entrenched mediocrity to stop it*

*The very idea that this was "equipment malfunction" is correct at one level, but at the management level, someone should have fixed it. Management was in effective.*

Links and References

# 12 Why Your Bank Closed Down

We're going to tackle the case of why your bank closed down, or in this case to be more precise, we're talking about your bank branch. This is the odd case of Wells Fargo Bank, which had to exit 20 states and close down a significant number of their branch offices because, as in a lot of these cases, there were multiple levels of people that didn't do their jobs.

The reason this is odd is that there is lack of agreement in the literature at the moment about who exactly it was that didn't do their job, which often happens in a big company like this.

## Back Story

The real back story starts in the "banking crisis" of 2008. For those unaware of the situation, this is what happened. A lot of banks went broke, because, unfortunately, the bankers that run them did not do their jobs in the two prior years.

The main problem was that "They" issued mortgage loans to a lot of people who had no business getting them, and bundled them together into what is called MBS or Mortgage-Backed Securities. This happened because the mortgage loan issuers themselves decided not to follow the standard operating procedure, which was to tell these people "No."

In case you missed it, yes, we're talking about the "Amorphous They" here, the mysterious people in any organization that have authority, but no accountability.

Then, "They" sold these "mortgage-backed securities" to various investors and other entities. Normally if one person has terrible credit, and you tried to sell a mortgage to the marketplace it needs to be done at a discount.

Do I need to explain this? Let's say that you are one of the independent mortgage companies, or banks that issue a mortgage for $100,000 for a 5% interest rate. The interest rate is the amount they charge for a credit-worthy customer to take out the mortgage. Banks, and especially mortgage companies sell these things into the marketplace. When they sell the mortgage to someone else, they do so at a "discount." This is to compensate the new owner for higher risk.

So, anybody that buys these at a discount pays a lower price for it, but they have to administer the loan, which is to say track down the mooch that doesn't pay.

https://youtu.be/WjIteY6Tvo4

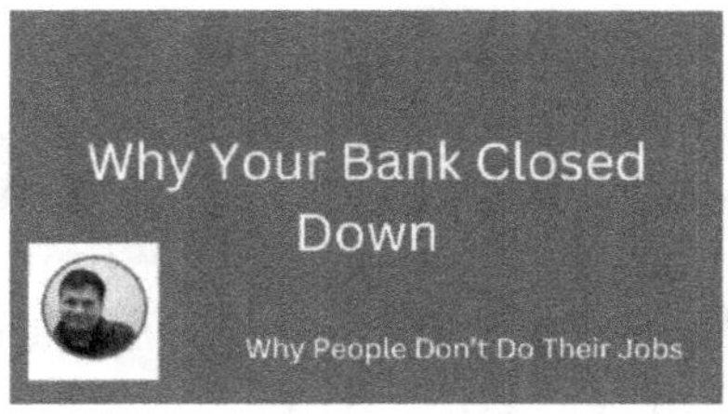


## More Back Story

At some point, the method was developed to bundle many of these mortgages together, and sell them as a "Mortgage-Backed Security."

These "bundled" mortgages are traded back and forth on the open market. The amount of risk in a mortgage-backed security is an aggregate of the risk of the individual mortgages, and determined by an independent third party.

The most famous one of these is Standard and Poor's bond rating service, whose job it is to determine how risky this thing is, and state publicly to the parties what is going on.

So, did Standard and Poor's and the other bond rating services do their jobs? Did they correctly raise the red flag, and provide the alarm system to the public that these MBS were terrible? **No, they did not.** The alarm system didn't work for some reason. In my opinion, that's why the whole thing happened. There were multiple layers in the system that didn't do their jobs, especially the people whose job it was to set the alarm.

A few bright people could see what had happened. They looked at some of these MBS, then went to some of these places to check them out, and could see right away by the furniture in the front yard that the loans were garbage.

The character Michael Burris knew all along that this was going to happen, and if you believe the movie "The Big Short" he withstood a lot of mental pressure from his investors because of this unorthodox opinion, which turned out to be right, making him fabulously rich while the whole system was collapsing.

What then happened was that the US Government stepped in and reset the system. They bailed out all of the banks that stupidly bought all of these bogus MBS, and made a lot of them consolidate. The less stupid banks bought the banks that had gone broke, and over the period of a year or two, the system was stabilized.

One of the "Surviving Banks" was Wells Fargo. They were always one of the nation's biggest banks, and in the 2008–2012-time frame was able to make themselves even bigger. They also got $25 Billion from the government because of their cooperation in bailing out the economy. These are the banks that are too big to fail that people are talking about.

No one went to jail, but some people did get fired, as we are about to see.

## Even More Back Story

This very famous bank, with a long history, was stable enough that the management thought they could expand. Their business strategy was to be a "one stop shop" for consumers, who they would then take in money, and collect a lot of bank fees and credit card interest.

So, for the period of 2012 through 2015, they embarked on an aggressive growth program.

Here is how it worked: The management decided to open as many locations as possible, and use various selling tactics to get consumers to open many accounts, and get as many bank-branded credit cards as possible.

This strategy was developed by the then-President John Stumpf, who "ran" the company between 2007 and 2016, and his evil hench-person Carrie Tolstedt. These people did not do their jobs. They belong in the "supervillain" category with a lot of authority, but little or no accountability, which you will see below.

## Implementation

Next, they opened a lot of branch offices, and started to ramp up the process of signing up customers. Carrie Tolstedt, who was on "Fortune" magazine's "most powerful women in banking" list, led the charge.

The idea was to underpay the staff at the branch banks, and make their pay based on commissions and rewards for signing people up for accounts. The number that was thrown out was that each customer was expected to have 6 accounts with the bank.

It was communicated to the employees that their job was to sign up as many people as possible. This is in contrast to the normal job of a bank, which is to keep peoples' money safe, and provide financial services that they actually want.

It is not clear anymore exactly what happened on this except that there was acceptance of this idea by literally thousands of middle managers and branch managers. They apparently either didn't see anything wrong with it, or were powerless to say anything. But suffice it to say, it worked.

A lot of accounts were started, including some that the customers didn't authorize. It got to the point where the employees started to sign up homeless people, and write fake accounts to meet their quota and get paid enough to live.

## Incentives

I have toyed with the idea of a chapter on incentives, i.e. "pay."

But instead, I will refer you back to the original book in this series, which has a chapter on dog training. No two employees are motivated by the same reward. It is also clear that a system is perfectly designed to produce what it does, and what that means is that the incentive systems in this business were set up to maximize the amount of corruption.

I would also refer you to the chapter on McCaig's Law, which says that nothing happens in isolation.

## Lawsuits and Other Peril

At some point in about 2016 all of this was publicly exposed, and the bank was in a heap of trouble, as they say out west. Various consumer protection services and the City of Los Angeles sued them. At one point, according to the article below, there were over 3.5 million fake accounts at this bank.

In about 2014, I myself went into one of these places to open a checking account, and ended up with 4 accounts. A savings account, a branded credit card that I cut up, and an ATM debit card which is also a credit card. The young branch sales person would have loved to have signed me up for more.  my personal experience is consistent with this.

The practice evidently still remains in the corporate culture. As of 2023 there were still some reports that customers were still being signed up without their consent.

Carrie Tolstedt was singled out for not doing her job by not monitoring all of this, or rather contributing to it.

## Aftermath

There is a nice story in the Links and References from Forbes which lists the fines, paybacks, class action suits, and refunds that Wells Fargo was required to pay. As part of a general retrenchment, which was accelerated due to Covid, they had to close a lot of branch offices.

Here, in fact, is the number of Wells Fargo branches per the respective years' annual reports, which I have linked in the links and references.

| Year | Number of Branches |
|---|---|
| 2017 | 8300 |
| 2018 | 7800 |
| 2019 | 7400 |
| 2020 | 6900 |
| 2021 | 6900 |

| 2022 | 4600 |
|---|---|

This is your story. This is the reason your bank closed down.

## Further Aftermath

Here is the real bottom line, since the job of the management is to maximize the wealth of the shareholders, here's a stock chart for Wells Fargo for the last five years. They've fallen behind their made competitor, Chase Bank, so their "strategy" didn't work, despite the "efforts".

By the way, I think everybody should be required to learn to read a financial statement as part of their education. If you care to read Wells Fargo's most recent one, you'll be able to tell how much all of this is still costing them, and how their "rebranding" project has been going, to try to get the marketplace to forget about all of this.

## Accountability

According to the articles I have linked, John Stumpf, in front of a congressional hearing, volunteered to pay $60 million of the $130 million of his Wells Fargo compensation. Carrie Tolstedt had to repay $63 million of her retirement cash-out but still got to "keep" $60 million. In 2020 she pleaded "Guilty" to the crime of obstructing an official investigation, and in March of 2023 she was sentenced to 2 years' probation to avoid jail time.

In both of these cases, they got to keep around $60 million, and did not have to go to jail.

Is that what you would call "accountability?" I will let you decide.

## The Ownership

I am also throwing this in for a reason. I've linked the major shareholders in Wells Fargo, Chase Bank and Bank of America.

Each of these three banks are 75-ish or so percent owned by institutional shareholders, the two main ones of which are Vanguard Group, and Black Rock, which are the two companies that, through their index funds, "own" about 15% of the national economy.

Is that an underlying cause? Well, it would be easy to theorize that because this is an inside group of people, it would be an option for a group of insiders to cherry pick officers and board members, despite them being evil. Or, maybe because they are evil.

That may be another reason these people didn't do their jobs.

Berkshire Hathaway, by the way, owned by Warren Buffett, has a position in Bank of America and not in the other two. Berkshire did have a position in Wells Fargo at one point, but since 2018 has unloaded it, correctly as it turns out.

## The Bottom Line

In short, here is why your bank shut down:

*Standard operating procedure was violated*

*Employee incentive programs were not aligned to be legal*

*Customers, shareholders and regulators were ticked off*

*Alarm systems and Accountability systems were weak or nonexistent.*

The end result, if you are one of the customers, is that in some states you can't find one of these banks at all, and in others, like mine, you need to stand in line a long time for anything. This is pretty much the opposite of good service, and all of it is a result of people not doing their jobs.

Links and References

# 13 Why Your Car got Recalled

This is the story of the largest automotive recall in history, and why your car got recalled.

The story has all of the classic elements of human failure, including not following the standard operating procedure, deliberately ignoring alarm systems, knowingly shipping and installing defective products, and covering the whole thing up with bribery and corruption.

There are also some low wage employees involved, along with entrenched mediocrity.

There is a little background information that we have to cover.

https://youtu.be/nlFzJjKOayY

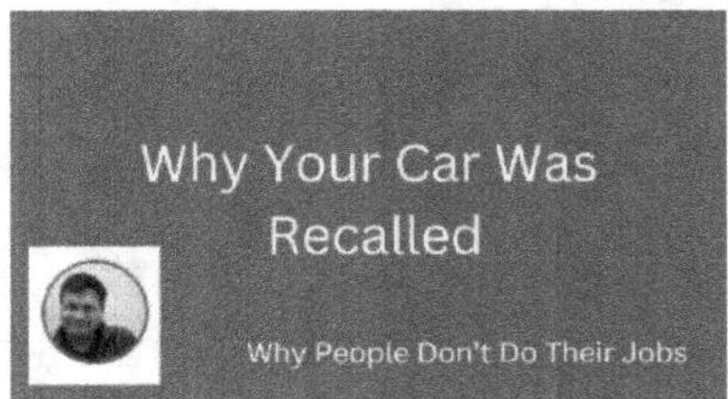

## OEMs and their Suppliers

We all know the Original Equipment Manufacturers. That's the industry insider name for the "car companies." What they actually are is "assemblers" who assemble components into a functioning vehicle. Why everybody doesn't just call them that is beyond me.

The layer of suppliers just below the OEM is called "Tier 1", better known as "Tier 1 Hell". The reason it is hell is because those poor people have a hard job. The system has evolved slightly differently in Japan as opposed to the USA, but it doesn't really matter, it's still "hell."

Being a Tier 1 supplier may possibly be a huge profitable activity, because of the sheer volume of purchases that the auto companies make. These are enormous, complicated operations, and nowadays, they're also expected to participate in engineering and development activities.

The way it works is that the "Tier 1" is often very intimate with the OEM. Very often, the OEM owns a significant portion of the suppliers' stock. In Japan, there is a whole bastardized system of interlocking ownership and banking, in which the participants all have an incestuous relationship. In the US it is not quite as obvious, but all of the US OEMs have their favorite suppliers and a lot of these are historical.

In Japan, this system is called "Keiretsu." I have included a reference.

What also happens is that there is an expectation of a price decrease every year between the supplier and the OEM. The underlying rationale is that as time goes on, the Tier 1 supplier is expected to get better at their jobs, and operate more efficiently, and pass savings down to the OEM.

There is also an expectation that the suppliers tell the OEM if they are making any kind of process change, so that they are aware of any potential issues, and also, can get a piece of the action from a pricing point of view.

Another reason this works is that the OEM's are able to shift some of their development costs upstream to the suppliers, thus making their own companies more "profitable." The expectations are lower on the part of the Tier 1 suppliers, and the Tier 2 suppliers below that.

## Tier 1 Hell

Anyway, from the point of view of the Tier 1 suppliers, and any suppliers below that, there is constant pressure to cut corners and reduce costs. Failure to do so will cost you the relationship with your OEM and quite likely the management and any employees involved will be fired.

So, as a result of this, there is an enormous incentive to lie and cheat, because it is easier than telling the truth. Price fixing is also a popular activity, and every few years there are arrests and fines for this.

Not only that but very often, some competitor will come in behind you with a similar product and cut your throat for a tenth of a cent per part.

There are a limited number of these huge companies that are under relentless pressure all the time.

It is a hard job, practically impossible to do properly.

## The Takata Airbag Company

This company was founded in Japan in 1933, and made a lot of money, making buckles for parachutes, which were popular at the time for some reason.

They shifted to automotive in the early 1950's and became the premier producer of the buckles and hardware on your seat belt. Selling a low-entry-barrier part into the Japanese OEM's was profitable at the time, and fit with the company's capabilities.

In the 1970's they expanded into infant seats, and other safety equipment, and eventually branched into steering wheel parts. They also had some business in interior electronics.

Takata started making airbags and inflation systems in 1988 and had about 20 percent of the marketplace for this type of product. This is where the story gets interesting. Faulty airbags were being placed in Hondas as early as 1994, and both companies knew about it and did not do anything about it.

In 1995 they were hit with their first product recall, when a lot of their seat belts didn't stay buckled in Toyotas and Hondas, and a $50,000 slap on the wrist was given to both Takata and Honda, for not coming clean on this issue.

In the 2013- and 2014-time frame, there were a lot of problems with the air bags. The law requiring air bags to be put in the front seats of cars in the US started in 1998. There were ongoing issues because it is a different problem to stop a 200-pound man and a 35-pound three-year-old with the same gadget. The way this is accomplished from a technical standpoint is to have a little inflator container with some explosive material in it. When the sensor on the car figures out that the car has been hit, the explosion happens and deploys the airbag.

## Cost Reduction

In 2013, Takata moved their main production facility for the inflator units to a plant in Mexico. This was done for only one reason, to reduce cost.

At the same time, they switched the explosive propellant. There is an interesting class lesson produced by the American Chemical Society that I have linked that will help explain this. What they ended up with is a chemical called "ammonium nitrate" which along with being a fertilizer, is the same stuff used to blow up the Murrah Federal Building in Oklahoma City.

The little explosion that inflates your air bag was not so little. There was sometimes shrapnel, some of which was lethal.

There were a couple of instances of people not doing their jobs in the plant in Mexico. First of all, the chemicals were not being properly stored, causing them to deteriorate. Secondly, there was a huge fire at one point that burned the place down. Could they possibly have a disengaged, ticked off, sick, exhausted workforce that can't understand warning labels in English or Japanese? I have only been in a couple of facilities in Mexico, and it was a while back, but suffice it to say that if I were any kind of investigator on this case, I would make this the starting point.

In retrospect, it was inevitable. A disengaged, lowly paid newly hired workforce and a really dangerous product. What could possibly go wrong?

## Denial, Corruption, and Intentional Neglect

In this time frame, the bribes and corruption started to fly, as did the lawsuits.

Takata knowingly conveniently "lost" a lot of production quality data that would have proven that the product was defective. They furthermore covered up test data, and stonewalled the investigation.

At the end of 2014 there was enough pressure, and enough major responsible car companies were recalling their products that the whole thing unraveled. At that point, in the US at least, the government regulators got involved and did a forced recall of all vehicles with these suspect air bags.

In 2017 some of the officers of the company were finally charged with negligence. The company was fined about $2B and nobody was happy about it. By 2018 the company could no longer function even in seat belts and the whole thing was sold out to someone presumably a little more honest.

So, to make a long story short, everybody knew, but the decision was made to produce these things for several years, and no one did anything about it. Three officers of the company wound up in jail over this.

Eventually 67 million of these inflator units were recalled, making it the biggest recall in history thus far.

Some of these cars have "do not drive" warnings, but according to sources, there are still a lot of these things rolling around up until today.

## What Keeps it from Happening Again?

Well, I guess after having reviewed all of this, you'd have to say it is very likely that the same thing will happen over and over because of the inherent strategy of this industry which forces people to do a lot of work without making money.

There will still be constant cost pressure, need to continually redesign things, and constant incentive to lie.

## The R and D People

The research and development people that developed all of this fell short of their goal of perfecting this technology, but based on the documents in the 43-page Congressional Report, they were quite open about this when they told management.

Things like this happen in R and D occasionally when the laws of physics bump up against the laws of economics. There is enormous incentive at all levels of the organization to fudge a little.

The R and D people in automotive, and also other industries, are very innovative. If challenged, they could create an infallible air bag mechanism, or tire, or windshield wiper if they had to. But they are constrained by three things: It can't be ugly, it can't be complicated to install into the vehicle, and it needs to be cheap. That being the case they can't "over-engineer" things to last forever. They need to "just right" engineer things to last a known length of time, on average.

To the extent that they are limited that way, the engineers can't do the job that everybody wants, because there are limits in the system.

## The Marketing Department

The marketing and high-level engineering people that presented the changes to the customers decided to cherry pick the data i.e. "lie" to the customers. These people didn't do their jobs, and the underlying reason is, they were in a system where honesty is expensive. Product delays could have meant the expenditure of millions of dollars in replacement shipments, and so they also took a calculated risk.

As it turns out, the calculated risk blew up in their faces literally. These are the entrenched and mediocre employees that are always walking the fine line between risk and reward.

There is a whole activity, namely Failure Mode Effects Analysis, (FMEA) that they're required to do for every component. After a while, these organizations know exactly how risky a design choice is going to be from the standpoint of safety.

But," they" go ahead and make bad decisions anyway because of the ongoing cost/benefit pressure in this industry. Are these "Amorphous They?" You'd better believe that these people thrive in this kind of organization.

Do you want an example? The lessons of the 1995 recall didn't filter down to this generation of employees 15 years later for some reason. One possible reason is, the culture within Takata was apparently such that this kind of behavior is tolerated because that's the industry they are in.

## Management

Somehow, the management of this company, Takata, got to be populated by people who prioritized profit over safety, and tolerated this form of entrenched mediocrity. No one in the organization could say "no" despite obvious technical risk.

How did this happen? We discussed this earlier on. It happened because people were promoted and advanced through the organization for reasons other than "character." This permeated all of the levels of the organization and became part of the culture.

Some real author would go back to the early stages of the development of this company and try to figure out the point at which it all went wrong. People got promoted into decision making positions, and were rewarded for making half-assed business decisions that got the company into a lot of trouble.

## The OEMs

The Honda process, and similar processes in other companies that are supposed to keep out the riff raff did not do its job. Here is how it is supposed to work: The change process is supposed to be very disciplined in this situation, to avoid exactly this kind of catastrophe. The supplier is supposed to go through a PPAP process (Production Part Approval Process) in which specimens are evaluated. The means of this evaluation is planned out well in advance, including determining exactly what it will take to pass the test and be approved.

And, even at that, there are limited production trials, and longer-term tests, and of course all of that takes time and money. So, when the OEMs approved this stuff based on Takata's data, that was probably a bad idea, and the gatekeepers didn't do their jobs.

It is very possible that they didn't pull the plug on Takata because they couldn't. In this industry because of keiretsu, they couldn't just kick the company out because changing suppliers would also have been enormously expensive and they are all in bed with each other. There was immense financial pressure to work with the supplier, and tolerate mediocrity.

## The Government

Did the government do their jobs? Unfortunately, all they can do is help regulate the mess, throw people in jail and give out fines and sentences. They may or may not have done a good job at all of that.

I am ready to say that the "recommendations for further action" in this case were somewhere between weak and useless.

The first recommendation was to "phase out" the suspect material, and gradually switch to something better. What that says is it is okay, Takata, you switch back when you get around to it. They may have had their reasons for doing this gradually. A better way would have been to have pulled the plug on it entirely, but that would have been inconvenient and expensive.

The second recommendation was to expedite the development of a better propellant. Can you see where that might not be the greatest idea without testing it first?

The last recommendation was to do a better job of managing the recall, and we can sort of agree to that in light of the fact that there are still plenty of cars on the road with these explosive airbags in them.

If you are a person who believes in the government being actively involved in this kind of thing, you'd have to be a little frustrated.

## The Plant in Mexico

I think I covered this already. The likelihood that this is a disengaged, ticked off, impaired workforce, managed by indifferent supervisors and managers is very high. You can't 100 percent blame them, however. The decision to produce these dangerous things in a less controlled environment is exactly the kind of thing the "Amorphous They" would have done.

Chances are, if you did a real investigation, you'd be hard pressed to find the exact person that decided to open up this place.

Also, regarding the plant: It's not up to them to get the kinks out of the project. In my experience, having been in a project like this once, you can't just bulldoze out a portion of real estate in a "developing country," construct a factory and hire a workforce and expect them not to blow up. Any startup like this has a lot of problems even if they're producing something harmless. You need to establish process procedures, and do a lot of training, and take some lumps.

So, whoever in management had the job of relocating this production operation could very well have shortcut safety procedures, undertrained the workforce, and failed to set up production conditions properly. We'll never know exactly, except in this industry, the temptation is strong to start things up before they are ready, because time is money.

## Why Your Call Got Recalled

So here is the bottom line on all of this. Your car got recalled because people didn't do their jobs, as follows:

*Standard operating procedures ref: product development processes were shortcut, allowing defective products to be installed in vehicles.*

*Alarm systems were broken. There was systematic effort to hide bad news, and once it was discovered, more systematic effort not to do the right thing.*

*The people in charge of all of this allowed it to go on despite obvious risk. That is one of the very definitions of entrenched mediocrity.*

*The systems in place to identify and fire the management and executives that were making these terrible decisions also failed.*

That about covers it. We should not get the warm and fuzzy feeling that the problem will never happen again, because it will. Maybe the airbags won't blow up, but something else will, and it's all part of the territory.

## Bonus Section for Math Nerds (Skip if you must.)

I had to get some entertainment from the little bit of raw data that was presented on page 11 of the congressional report that I have linked in the links and references. It gives two sets of data, the original data which was generated by TKH which is the US part of the operation, and TKJ which was the Japan part.

Here is the summary:

| | Original | Fudged |
|---|---|---|
| Average | 54.52 | 54.32 |
| St Dev | 3.16 | 2.56 |
| 3-sigma | 64 | 62 |
| Burst Pressure | 94 | 94 |
| Safety Factor | 1.46875 | 1.51612903 |
| Prob Upper Limit | 0.0021 | 0.0008 |
| Probability Max | 0.0013 | 0.0001 |
| N | 67,000,000 | 67,000,000 |
| Failures, Upper Limit | 140,700 | 53,600 |
| Failures, Max | 87100 | 6700 |

| Z Score | 12.5 | 15.5 |
|---|---|---|

The problem was that when the propellant was exploding, it was exceeding the burst strength of the little container. The burst strength was determined to be 94 MPa, and the average strength of the explosion was around 54 MPa.

But because of the variability of the process, sometimes it is more or less than 54 MPa. If the explosion is too forceful, the maximum burst strength would be exceeded, and there would be shrapnel going into someone's head.

So that's the standard deviation. About ⅔ of the time, the results fall within one standard deviation of 54 MPa or from about 57 to 51, since the standard deviation is 3.16 in the first case and 2.52 in the second case.

They set the factory limit usually at what is called 3-sigma. That's three times the standard deviation, or in this case 64 or 62. The "safety factor" of 1.5 was put in that says this: we're going to set up this system such that the very top of the factory limit was 50% below the burst strength. So that's your safety factor.

## Engineering Overkill

The "data fudging" occurred in that the engineers threw out and/or adjusted data so that the population average was about the same, but the variability was lower. That made the safety factor look like it was just above 1.5 which was apparently the limit. Sometimes these limits are set by the customer, or are "generally accepted." and the more critical the item is, the higher this limit is.

That, for want of a better term, is your "engineering overkill."

Does the difference between 1.47 and 1.51 really matter to anyone? It is negligible from a practical standpoint.

## Risk Acceptance

Using this data, and knowing that 67 million of these things were produced, you can calculate the approximate number of failures you could expect when they're sent out into the world.

Using the 3-sigma factory limit, in the first case, you can expect about 140,000 failures, and in the second case, only about 50,000, due to the reduced variability. That's one reason that they lied. They wanted that number to be as small as possible because that's the known accepted risk of these things getting out into the world, even though it's just a statistical calculation.

No matter where you set the upper limit in the factory, a certain fraction of these things is going to be higher than 94. In the first case, it's around 87.000 and in the second case, supposedly it's only 6,300. Does that number mean anything? Someone that doesn't understand math might worry about it, but the reality is that the test itself isn't that accurate. Also, it's still just a statistical prediction. Merely changing the testing conditions might reduce that number by a few thousand.

The real risk of one of these things blowing up and killing someone is lower than that, of course. If you consider that most cars never get into a wreck in their lifetime, those that do usually don't deploy the airbag, an even smaller number of these actually were involved in fatalities.

In fact, only 27 fatalities have been reported due to exploding air bag shrapnel. You can never reduce the risk all the way to zero.

But, to them, why was it that important that the risk factor be just over, rather than just under, 1.5?

Here is my theory: Their competitors lied, or quite possibly the customer's purchasing people lied.

## This Happens A Lot

This sort of thing used to happen to me all the time. Part of my job at one point was to do this sort of development and try to sell it to a customer. The purchasing agent used to say "Your competitor can give me a price of X and a safety factor of 1.51 which is greater than my limit of 1.50. So, you have to beat that in order to do business with me.

I, the development engineer had no way to validate whether the purchasing agent was lying or not, except yes, I did. I would obtain samples of the competitors' material and test them, and they were no better than mine, and I knew that.

https://youtu.be/v6T3yf9An4Q

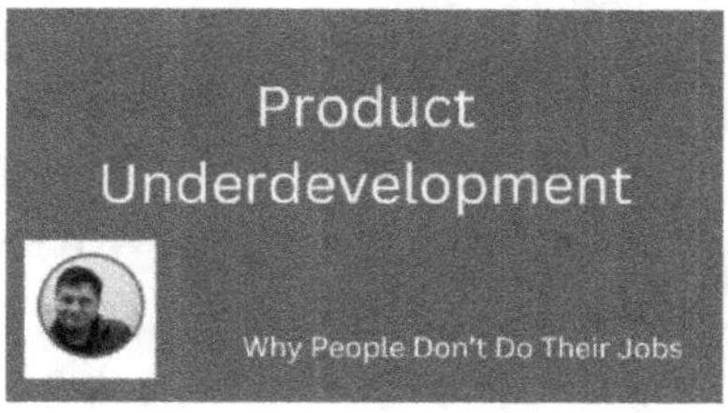


Either my competition lied, or the purchasing agent lied, so as to get a better price.

What that did was either encourage me to lie, or make me walk away from the business, because I was not able to achieve that level of uniformity with my current materials and equipment at that price. My management was unwilling to go below a certain price because they also had their business needs. My production equipment was sort of limited i.e. "junky."

So that's the dilemma, and this sort of thing happens in automotive all the time. The financial stakes are so huge for both companies, that there is enormous incentive to lie.

Even if I were to go back into the purchasing department and tell them that I sampled the competitive product and found out it was no better, I would be dismissed.

That's because, in a lot of cases, there was bribery, kickbacks, or forms of "persuasion" that were going on all the time in the background that I was only vaguely aware of. This goes double in a place that is into the keiretsu situation where these supplier/customer relationships are tainted by interlocking management and ownership structures.

## Do I blame them?

We've arrived at a possible other instance of why people don't do their jobs, which is that there is a culture that is so corrupt that actually doing your job works against you. This is entrenched corruption, and I guess we can write another book at some point, starting with this instance as a pattern.

In this particular case, the recalls and lawsuits literally bankrupted the company. I don't know how much more expensive the alternate propellant was, and how much money per part was saved by doing a bad job on this, and lying about the data.

I'll be willing to bet that it was less than the value of the company, and it probably wasn't worth it.

## It's Complicated

In the grand scheme of things, the failure of these airbags, as a fraction of the production, is actually negligible in either case. If your smartphone worked at that level of reliability, you would love it. But you can't really tell that to Congress, when the press gets involved. "Why doesn't someone do something?" the frantic moms will ask.

The owners and managers of the company, and newspaper reporters who don't know anything about statistics, are making decisions and forming opinions on the basis of these numbers all the time. We're going to see another case shortly about that very thing.

Politicians, accountants, corporate weasels, and everybody else that sees that data won't appreciate it for what it is. There is no such thing as "risk free."

I always used to say "the world is full of chaos and there are no guarantees on anything" and that is actually the case.

Links and References

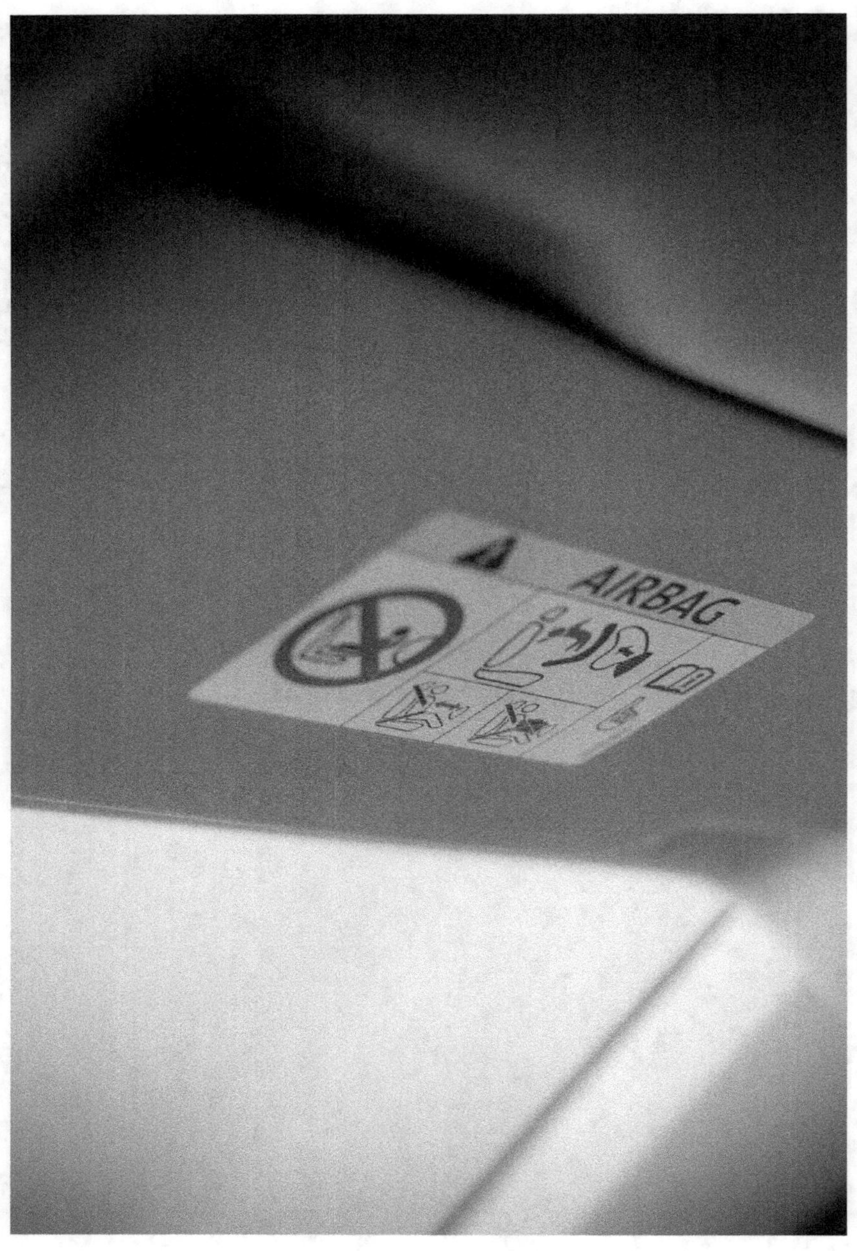
AIRBAG

# 14 How to Bankrupt a Famous Company

Along the lines of the last chapter, we're now going to learn how to bankrupt a famous company. The company was once one of the most famous companies in the nation, ranked 35th in the Fortune 500, and within a couple of decades was effectively bankrupt, had to lay off 65,000 employees, and had to sell out to a competitor to keep the value of its branding.

We should be able to apply the same lessons we learned regarding people not doing their jobs, if we can possibly figure out which of the "Amorphous They" is responsible for the disaster.

Plus, as in the previous case, the lessons were so poorly learned by the people involved at the time, they were repeated about 20 years later, with even more disastrous results.

It's about Firestone. I and a lot of other people used to work there.

## Harvey S. Firestone

Let's talk about this fellow first, because it's important to the story. Harvey Firestone was a farm boy from Columbiana OH and was selling buggy tires up around the Great Lakes, in the year 1898.

He stumbled into the shop of Henry Ford, in Dearborn, sold Henry a set of tires for his new invention, and on the basis of a handshake, began a partnership that made both men among the wealthiest in the history of the country within 20 years.

If you want to go back to the chapter where we were talking about the Family Business and other forms of business development, you can do so. This fellow was obviously the "driver."

Harvey was interested in improving tires themselves, and when he started the Firestone Tire and Rubber Company, he was a technological innovator and pioneered the pneumatic tire, the detachable tire (so that it could be repaired) and replaced the clunking old metal tractor wheels with pneumatic rubber agricultural tires.

His relationship with Ford and Thomas Edison was so close that the three used to go camping every summer, famously with whoever was the President of the US at the time.

According to the reference I have linked, Harvey was a bit the concierge. Helped pitch the tents, fry up whatever they fried for breakfast, and that kind of thing.

I found a reference to a lot of his quotes. Based on this, an echo from the past, this fellow was humble, knew how lucky he was, knew how hard it was to make and keep customers, and sounds like a rather nice fellow.

Here's my favorite one:

**"If anything in the business is wrong, the fault is squarely with management."**

Firestone Family Farm Video

https://youtu.be/WGFr_MaE2rY

Here's another good one:

**I believe fundamental honesty is the keystone of business.**

## Taking care of Employees

He had also adopted a lot of Ford's ideas about taking care of the workforce. He introduced the 8-hour day, paid people generously, and the Firestone Country Club was open to all employees when it was constructed.

For that brief period in history, the entrepreneurs, being farm boys themselves, appreciated the fact that they got lucky and felt sort of a paternal bond with the labor force. That is also important to the story, as we will see later.

In 1932, he handed control of the then-massive Firestone Company to a born executive, Harvey S. Firestone Jr.

## Harvey S. Firestone Jr.

This might be the more interesting fellow. He was born in a 114-room mansion, and spent his time being literally the Great Gatsby. He managed to graduate from Princeton in 1920, and was named "most likely to succeed." He joined the company in 1926. Reportedly he liked polo and alcohol.

He was behind the purchase of more than 10% of a significant country in Africa, where he got into bed with the local warlord, and worked people under near -slave-labor conditions. There is some historical revisionism by Princeton, who received large donations, the story of which is linked in the links and references.

He later quadrupled the sales of the company by being a war profiteer, and in the period after the war, started to produce missiles and various other weapons of destruction for the US Government.

He was a main figure behind the very hostile Rubber Workers Strikes in 1937 and 1946, which made the company's relationship with the workforce violent and angry.

The best one was in 1950, after he was named President.

Who framed Roger Rabbit

https://www.youtube.com/watch?v=zpaf-O1pY6Q

You remember this scene from "Who Framed Roger Rabbit?" Well, it actually happened, and it was Firestone, Goodyear, and Standard Oil who actually bought the Red Car system.

## McCaig's Law, Practically Applied

On the surface of it, you'd have to say he was obsessed by out-doing the old man, in one way or another. But, as we have pointed out, nothing happens in isolation. We all know that the view of the Boss takes over the business. People get promoted into management on the basis of what they think. There is some question as to whether anybody can say "no."

Pretty soon this whole mindset, of maximizing sales and profits at the expense of everything else, was contagious.

On top of that, during the period right after the War, a lot of these employees were hired with a military background, and positions were filled with people who were used to following orders. If the boss ordered you to do something, even if it was questionably ethical or life-threatening, you would do it. Harvey Jr. had been in WW1 as a pilot, naturally, and along with being rich, you can imagine he would have a hard time with anyone telling him "No."

For reference, I would refer you to the life story of E. H. "Buck" Strobel, which I have linked. This fellow, ex-military, was put in charge of tire development in 1970, and was known as the "Father of the Firestone 500" which needless to say was not put into his obituary but probably should have been as a lesson to the future.

So, we're building our cast now. We have the Great Gatsby, a Top Gun Pilot, who would cut ethical corners to maximize profits, and a dutiful crew of do-or-die subordinates. What could possibly go wrong?

## Discontinuous Change

Prior to about 1970, the dominant construction of tires was "Bias Ply." I will not bog you down with too much technical detail on this.

Here is Harvey Senior himself building one. The uncured tire was hand assembled on a collapsible drum, and when it came off, it was taken to a clamshell tire press, where it was inflated into the inside of a very hot mold, where the tread design was put into it.

At the end of the process, the tire popped out and it looked like a tire.

It used to be my job, among other things, to go and check the pressure at which this would happen. This involved getting my head right next to a 370-degree mold, and confirming that the tire was being inflated properly, while at the same time, superheated steam was being pumped into a quarter inch thick rubber bladder which did the inflation.

It was a bit dangerous.

## Radialization

"Radial Tires" were invented back in the early days of tires, but were never commercially viable, because of their increased cost until the mid-1960's, which coincided with the popularity of "muscle cars" and other high-performance vehicles.

The first commercial agreement to produce and sell tires was between Michelin and Sears, in 1965.

By 1970, Ford, who was still Firestone's biggest customer, insisted that radial tires be commercialized. There were disruptive performance advantages to radial tires. They would last three times as long, and give better handling and fuel efficiency. But at the small scale, they were deemed too expensive for original equipment.

The prevailing attitude at Firestone was "It's just a fad" and "no one will put these on their station wagon."

There is an interesting article from the Harvard Business Review which I shall quote:

*Firestone's reliance on managers' existing strategic frames and values and the company's processes proved counterproductive in a changing competitive environment.*

There used to be a TV commercial, with a couple of technicians in lab coats dumping glass bottles in front of a speeding car equipped with radial tires. I can still remember vividly the crusty old quality control manager where I worked coming into a big employee meeting and telling us that the cheapest Deluxe Champ bias ply tires would do exactly the same thing, and that "Steel is No big Deal."

To be perfectly fair, Harvey Jr. was out of the scene at the time, and the place was being run by an "executive committee" of some kind, led by people that knew Harvey Jr.

https://youtu.be/syv4smQrxok

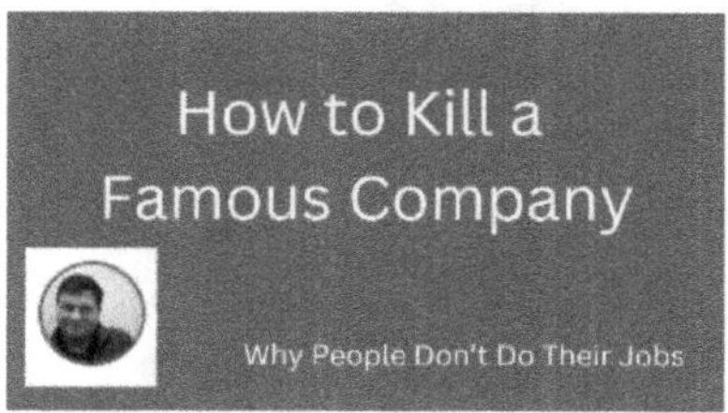


## The Problem with Radials

Here it is. Imagine the Michelin Man, a big, doughy ball of goo, standing between two plungers. These plungers squeeze him into the mold so that the tread design would go around his belly. Well, Bibendum himself represented the proverbial Bias Tire which would expand whatever way you wanted to squeeze it. The two plungers would come down, and Bib would be squeezed into the mold no problem to get the tread design and end up five inches tall

So then imagine Bibendum with a belt, like the one you use to hold your pants up, around his waist. It'll stretch a little, but not enough so that Bib can be squeezed out into the mold.

You obviously have to find some way to partially inflate the fluffy white guy, apply the belt and the tread compound, and then put the tire into the press, which is similar to a round waffle iron.

## Solving the Problem

What Firestone eventually decided to do is to try to do this on the cheap. They would use their old time Bias machines, like the one Harvey was using above, and make a two-stage tire.

You could build the carcass, and then on a second machine, inflate it, and apply the steel belts and the tread over the whole thing. That way, you could solve the problem without retooling the whole thing from scratch.

What happened was that you had a hard time maintaining the inventory control, since you had to have a certain number of "stage 1" tires to complete the "stage 2."

There were huge roomfuls of expensive racks of partly finished tires stacked to the ceiling, getting dirty and attracting moisture. Part of my job for a while was to track these things down and make sure people were doing first-in-first-out so that none of them got stuck in a dark corner somewhere.

To complete the process, the tire builder had to get the tread plies on perfectly straight, because if he didn't, the tires were out of round and wouldn't run straight. The solution to this problem was to trim about 1/4 inch off of each edge of the steel-reinforced belt, which was wasteful.

Then, you had to get the whole thing to hold together, in an awkward position, until you got it to the tire mold.

Then, you still had to stretch the tire out into the mold to get the tread pattern on it, and if you did that, it would have to stretch uniformly or the tread plies would move around, causing inconsistent rolling.

Then, once the tire came out of the mold, you had to do something called "post inflation" to make sure that it retained its shape, since its natural tendency was to shrink.

Then, the apparent fatal flaw was that they found out that as the tires were sitting in the warehouse, the complicated inorganic bonding agent they use to stick the rubber to the steel in the steel belts started to fail.

The tires passed the QC tests just fine when they were fresh, but when they aged a couple of months, they did not pass them just fine.

## The Better Way

There are alternative methods. Here's a video:

Michelin Radial Tire Production

https://www.youtube.com/watch?v=nFLQU17e31M

The fun stuff happens at about 3:00, where the tire is partly inflated prior to the tread plies being applied. All of this is done essentially robotically now. At the time, there was a sweaty tire builder hand-building these things, putting fingerprints and foreign material on everything. The job was paid "piece work" which meant that they were encouraged to be as fast as possible. More than once there would be a big wad of chewing tobacco cured into a tire, since the workforce was hostile, and allowed to chew tobacco all night.

## The Inevitable Failure

According to the HBR article, the estimate to retrofit the existing plants to Radial Tires, plus build a new Radial Only tire plant came to $140 million. There was a series of executive committee meetings in 1972, and the part about "building a new radial-only plant" sort of got lost in the shuffle. This is the work of the "Amorphous They" who also causes people to forget otherwise sound decisions.

"They" eventually ended up spending about $60 million and the focus was spent on converting the existing technology.

I witnessed the ground level effects of this in the plant.

What then happened was the Firestone 500, which became the most recognized brand in tires by 1974.

By 1977, 16 million tires were recalled when they started to fail on the highway. The "Adjustment Rate" which is the field failure rate of these things that required them to be replaced, was on the order of 17% compared to 5% for "normal tires."

Deaths were reported, the lawsuits started to fly, and the company was forced to recall all of them.

My part of this was, one dark and lonely night, to haul production records out of the basement of the plant and into a semi-trailer, to be used in the lawsuits. A lot of these records were paper, fragile, and a mess because they were in the basement but we went through a few of them. Some of them depicted tires whose treads lifted completely off, along with cars wrecked out in a ditch when this happened.

## The Aftermath

The initial instinct on the part of the management to stonewall the whole thing. They knew as far back as 1972 that there were issues with product reliability. In 1976, a US Government investigation happened, that quietly went away for some reason.

It was reignited in 1978, and by 1979 these things were recalled. It was also my job on occasion to go down to the receiving dock and cut the serial numbers out of the tires to make sure no one tried to put them on a vehicle.

At some point, the stockholders insisted that sanity take over. They put a finance guy, John Nevin, in place, and he moved the corporate HQ to Chicago to get away from the culture of mediocrity.

Since radial tires lasted three times as long, it meant that there only needed to be ⅓ as many factories, and factories throughout this industry were closed.

65,000 Firestone workers were laid off, plants were closed, and ultimately the retail stores and leftovers were sold to the Bridgestone Corporation, in 1988.

## Why People Don't Do Their Jobs–Company Killing Version

So, it's pretty clear what happened:

*The workforce was ticked off and/or impaired*

*The standard operating procedure was screwed up (development of the process was insufficiently validated and tested.)*

*The alarm systems, particularly the one that said "we have to quit selling these things" were broken. No one could pull the plug. Or, to put it more correctly, there was no process by which the plug must be pulled.*

*Money and resources were spent inadequately*

*The entrenched, mediocre management, selected for their lack of creativity, doubled down on production making the problem worse.*

So, whose fault is any of this? In the little video I made a few years ago, I sort of blamed Harvey Sr. for building an organization that ultimately killed the company, starting with putting his son on the board.

Harvey Jr. the "villain" built the actual organization. Maybe he has the blame. The organizational culture was such that no one could pull the plug, despite obvious risk, which is one of the several definitions of Entrenched Mediocrity.

## Side Information

I thought about not throwing this information in, but it sort of adds to the story about corporate culture.

In the five years I worked there, there were four workplace fatalities, and a suicide. A significant number of the employees had been maimed at some point: missing digits or worse from being stuck in some production equipment. The typical reaction of the plant management was to promote them to supervisor. There was actually a protocol for when someone died on the job. A black flag was flown in front of the plant.

Nowadays, they would try to do something about what killed the worker.

"Industrial Hygiene" was not a thing. Dust fires in the drums that captured the dust from the grinding equipment happened several times a week.

There were two bullet holes in the transom over the doorway where the Salaried employees worked, which were put there during the strike of 1976.

The classic story was that one night there was a hellacious thunderstorm at shift change, and the union clock workers, who had to park in a parking lot a quarter mile away from the entrance, had to walk through the guard house. To keep from getting drenched, they rooted through the garbage bins and found some scrap plastic film which they used as ponchos.

When they got to the guard shack, which was about halfway there, the guards made them give the "makeshift ponchos" back.

That was the culture. Would you send your kids to work in a place like that? There are more stories, which will have to wait for another book.

In the meantime, let me leave you with this additional term, which is **"Active Inertia."** This is where an organization works very hard to avoid change. In this case, they put an enormous amount of time and money into a technology and didn't face reality. We will talk about denial later.

## Further Idiocy

In 1995, this company was involved in another recall situation, which also resulted in multiple rollovers and fatalities, related to the Ford Explorer.

In that incident, which is one of the top 10 Automotive recalls in history, essentially the same thing happened.

The Ford Explorer was experiencing rollover problems at highway speeds. The cause was determined to be the Firestone tires, which were originally designed for some other vehicle with a lower center of gravity.

The company determined that rather than replace the tires with some other more expensive model, they would talk Ford into reducing the inflation pressure. This allowed the vehicle to ride a couple of inches lower. But, in so doing, the tires ran hotter, and some of them started to fail, making the problem worse.

By 2000, the government got involved again, and the whole thing led to the recall of 14 million tires in 2001.

Eventually the corporate culture of obfuscation, denial, and ignoring the problem precipitated the recall. The Decatur Illinois plant which had survived the crisis in 1978 was closed to stamp out any remnants of that culture, and things have now stabilized. Temporarily, at least.

Here's a quote:

*There were several primary causes for the tread separations: tire age, manufacturing facility, operating temperature, tire design, as well as labor and management problems in Bridgestone/Firestone and at the Decatur, Illinois factory.*

Here is another quote:

*Bridgestone pressured Firestone to cut manufacturing and labor costs to improve revenues. Critics and workers claim that this led Firestone to cut corners on production and to allow substandard tires to pass inspection that should have been rejected. This also led Firestone to pressure workers to accept new labor contracts that reduced pay and benefits and increased the hours that its factories were operating.*

At least in this case, the Presidents of Bridgestone/Firestone US and Bridgestone Corporation in Japan were fired, so it is true that there was some accountability.

## What Did We Learn from This?

Well, as Deming would still say, a system is perfectly designed to produce the outcome that it does. In this case, an organization was put together that was so internally focused, and so entrenched, that it allowed both of these problems to happen. This did not happen overnight, and there is obviously a lot of blame to go around, if you seek blame.

What we did learn is that there are common threads in all of these disasters, to whatever extent that makes them avoidable.

Or not. People not doing their jobs is part of the human condition sometimes.

Links and References

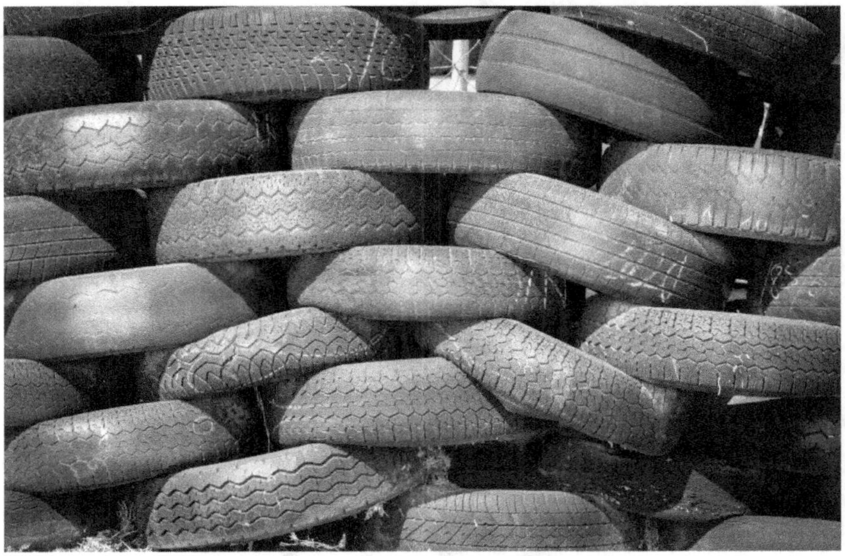

# 15 How to Bankrupt a Different Famous Company

This is the story of how to bankrupt a different famous company. This formerly respected company used to be the world's largest retailer, and now, the subsidiary in Mexico wants to change the name of the remaining stores to avoid the stink of failure.

And, it is the story of a fellow who was brilliant at one thing, but reached his level of incompetence at another thing, just like Peter predicted.

The company is the Sears Roebuck company, and the fellow's name is Eddie Lampert

https://youtu.be/xEXPpXJ9dJM

## Historical Context

The Sears Roebuck Company started in 1892 as a mail order company. It was a blessing for the farmers and others in rural areas who wanted to get "city" goods delivered to them.

It worked like this: Using the best communication method of the day, a customer could order an immense variety of items from a catalog. The order would be shipped and delivered in the most advanced transportation system of the day.

Does this sound familiar? It should. It's the Amazon business model.

This was so beloved in rural America that a song was written about it.

Wells Fargo Wagon ref: The Music Man

https://youtu.be/RRsv8ZhGa_E

By 1910 the company had over $50 million in sales, from its 322-page catalog, and by 1925, the company decided to diversify into brick-and-mortar stores.

The stores were located away from the city centers, had innovative store designs, and used advanced retailing methods. Among other things, they started to issue a "Christmas Catalog" which included items such as a kit to build the famous Craftsman houses.

By 1962 the company was so successful that it was selling more plows than John Deere, and was forced to spin off its subsidiary for lawn equipment by the FTC.

Between 1906 and 1972, a $1 investment in Sears Roebuck stock grew to $928, and with dividend reinvestment, grew to $9915, which would be an average rate of return of 11%, despite the Depression and two world wars that happened in that time frame.

The company tried to diversify into credit cards, brokerage services, and real estate, and made other attempts to diversify away from their main business, which was selling toilet seats to farmers.

At about the time the Sears Tower was completed in Chicago, the company reached its ironic peak.

## Ignoring Market Conditions

There are better sources than me for more information on why Sears was struggling, ironically what made them strong in the first place was now an Achilles heel.

The best article I saw just attributed it to hubris. The management lost focus on retail, the company neglected its stores, the product lines did not meet customer expectations, and the management was disengaged.

When that happens at the high levels, it permeates all the way down to the sales floor.

By the early 1990's Sears had been overtaken by Wal-Mart as the nation's largest retailer, and there began a steady decline.

## The Last Time I Shopped at Sears

I had to go to Columbus. I took a cab from the airport to the hotel, which was at the edge of town, and decided to replace my belt, which was rather ratty. I walked to the shopping mall next door, and went into Sears, on the theory that they should at least have a belt.

This was at about 4 PM on a Monday afternoon.

I made my selection, which was about $5 more expensive than the last belt I got at Wally Mart, and tried to find a cash register.

At Sears, the cash registers were located in the middle of the sales floor, unlike at Wally where they are close to the exit. I was able to find one, but it was deserted. I walked all around the store, stepping over boxes that were in the aisles, and found another one, where the rather indifferent clerk was struggling to get his register to work.

Cash register is down. Sorry. Come back later.

I finally just orphaned my purchase and walked out without buying anything, annoyed.

My last K-Mart purchase was roughly that bad. I can't remember exactly what it was, but after waiting in line for 20 minutes for the lone cashier to work through a group of noisy customers, I'd had enough.

Retail is detail, as the experts say.

## Enter Eddie Lampert

In 2004 a hedge fund run by Eddie Lampert, bought Sears, and merged it with K-Mart. Total cost was in the neighborhood of $11 billion

Hedge funds, for your information, buy things, extract the value, and then sell the pieces, or so they hope. They are not typically in a business for the long haul. But for whatever reason, it was Lampert's stated policy to try to revive the combined businesses into household names by competing against Wal Mart.

Here's a graph of the stock price.

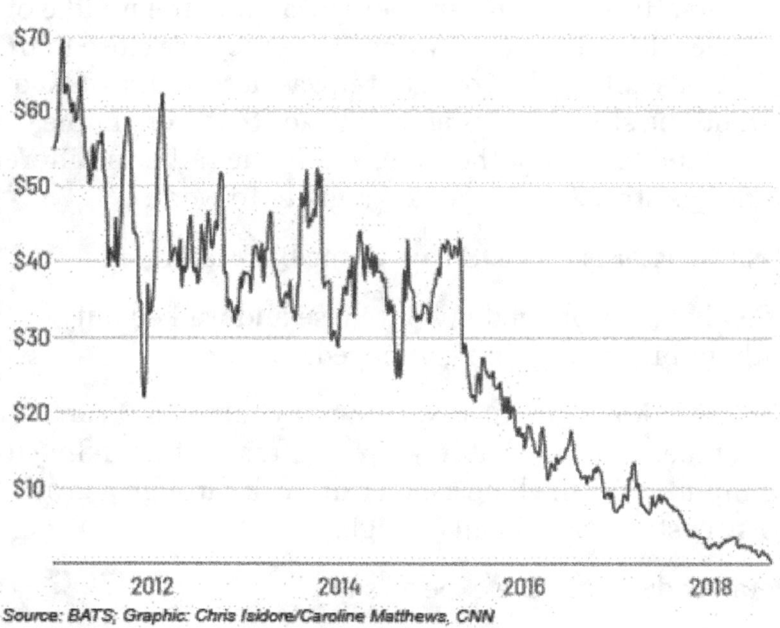

Sears customers had brand loyalty for Kenmore and Craftsman brands of appliances. There were some auto service stores, and some specialty retail stores that were selling lawn mowers and that kind of thing. So, there were a few positives. There was also some legacy real estate value in the whole thing.

There was no real reinvestment in the customer experience, and sales steadily declined.

Sears and Kmart Customer Experience

https://youtu.be/Qws713t3HBY

The "real" problem, according to the TV Talking heads, was that Lampert was not engaged in retail, never shopped in his own stores, and was a money man who didn't really have much interest in operations.

Sears Liquidation Announcement

https://youtu.be/-4IyYHRCrtA?si=LNkEnYoke4RXlokq

And, as a result of lack of engagement of the management, the stores were "terrible."

That was pretty much it. The company declared bankruptcy in 2018, and Eddie Lampert is still licking his wounds.  According to Forbes, his own personal net worth took a significant hit, and his reputation as a genius investor is now mocked.

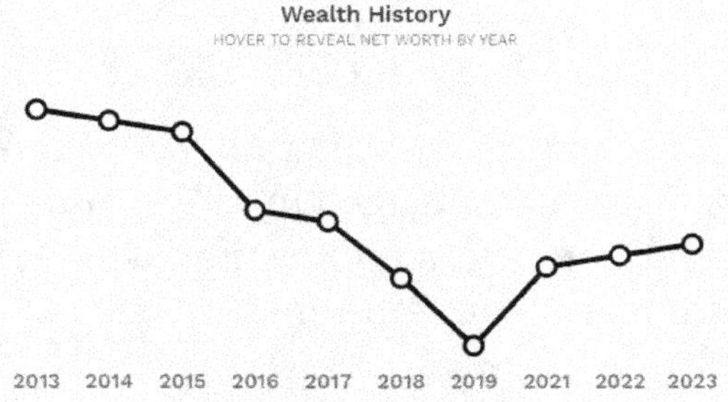


If your job is to maximize the wealth of the stockholders, this fellow did not do his job. He may yet make money on licensing the Kenmore name, but he ended up losing a fortune and it very nearly sunk him.

## Rhetorical Question

When a chain of stores is "terrible" who didn't do their job?

Is it the poor clerks and cashiers that actually have to stock the shelves or deal with the customers? No, of course not. As we said awhile back the low-authority high accountability people are the most remote from this. These are low wage workers.

Is it the store manager? No, these poor people are "survivors" of the whole retail management trauma. They don't get well paid, and they are very limited because of the corporate branding and pricing requirements. They can't change anything in the stores. Their main job is to try to retain staff, and restock. Hours are terrible. Customers complain. There are landlords. This is a hard job.

I'd go out on a limb and say that it's "They" who didn't do their jobs. These are the faceless people in "corporate branding." There is a whole activity in the main office that sits around and decides on what products to stock, how to present it in the stores, the signage, and everything else. They had no accountability if the whole thing turned into a disaster. Well, that is not exactly true. It was a disaster and they ended up unemployed.

But they didn't have to staff the stores, and take care of customers.

Target is doing a good job of this right now. Their stores are pleasant, everyone is in a nice red shirt, and the items look appealing.

## So here is your real problem

The Sears and K-Mart people were terrible at this when Lampert bought the place. Did he then spend money to bring in experts at branding and try to fix it? No, the indication is that because of all of the debt, and the bleeding of cash, he opted not to do that.

The fast-food people do these rebranding and store refurbishment projects all the time just to keep the stores fresh and pleasant. If they don't, they get dated and nasty.

Walmart just spent $500 million to upgrade 117 stores. Since they are committed to their business, they are always doing upgrades, closing "non-growing stores" and building new stores to keep the look fresh.

If you are Eddie Lampert and don't have the cash to do all of that, you're falling behind. You could have hired a "Brand Manager" and a whole staff of "Brand Strategy Associates" to develop pleasant stores and implement the design plans. You needed more "Technocrats" that knew what they were doing and didn't accept the legacy designs and branding.

They had no "corporate identity" that anyone liked.

## Transitioning to E-Commerce

While we're talking about changing, the further question comes up: Why did they not embrace E-Commerce, since they invented this business?

In the opinion of "Active Web Group" they had problems because their customer base, which was a lot of little old ladies, didn't use E-Commerce. There's your actual problem, they couldn't attract "young" customers.

The company couldn't switch demographics fast enough.

## The Aftermath

In 2022, a shareholder lawsuit was settled out of court for a mere $175 Million. There are still a few lawsuits out there floating around now, the most famous one is Simon Properties, who is the mall developer, who is trying to extract some unpaid rent from Lampert.

There was another $215 million lawsuit from the shareholders in 2006 which was settled as well.

It's a shame that Lampert's company is privately held, because if it was public, we would be able to get a list of lawsuits.

Meanwhile there are a lot of zombie stores in the country, and a lot of people that were put out of work awhile back but maybe that whole thing has faded into the past at this point.

## How to Bankrupt a Famous Company?

The process for renewing the stores was a failure because of lack of resources, you'd have to say. Whoever was in charge of this did not do their job.

Either that or the management was disengaged, and didn't realize what an unpleasant shopping experience the stores were, and it was nobody's job to fix it.

From Eddie Lampert's point of view: Did he do his job?

First of all, was he correctly placed as an expert in retail management? I'd have to say that despite the success as a hedge fund manager, he had no business doing this project.

The standard operating procedure for retail? Refurbishing the stores and doing branding? You'd have to say this was a failure as well.

The resources? There was not enough cash to do this job justice, you would have to say, the stores themselves were nasty.

Alarm systems? Here's another apparent problem. He didn't realize that the situation was that bad because he never went to Sears, nor did anyone else, and there was no internal system to tell him this information. "Hubris" in this case is all about not understanding customers and customer feedback.

There's your failure story.

Links and References

# 16 Technostress

Technostress is a negative psychological relationship between people and the introduction of new technology. I am ready to say that it applies to an organization just as much as it applies to an individual human.

In this era, "sorry our server is down" is a common lame excuse used by people who can't or won't do their jobs.

In either case, we're talking about an "unsuitable technological environment" which causes organizational dysfunction.

https://youtu.be/BDPNpuPT568

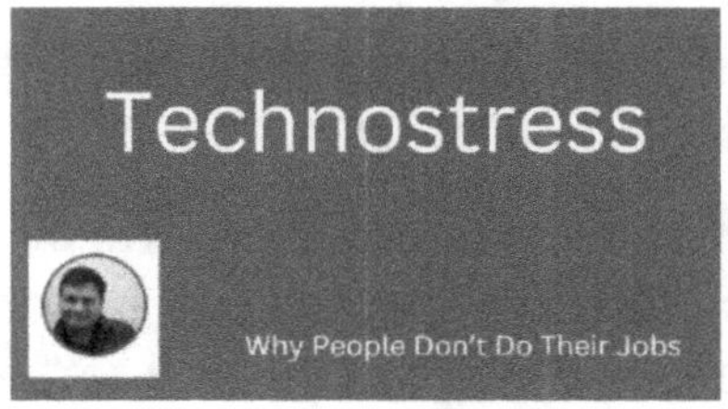

## Symptoms of Technostress

It turns out that there are actual physical symptoms associated with Technostress, which may include eyestrain, backaches, neck and back pain, dry mouth and stomach discomfort.

Other symptoms may include high blood pressure, irritable bowel syndrome, and difficulty breathing.

There may be emotional symptoms. These may include anger, emotional aspects like irritability, loss of temper, having a high state of anxiety when separated from a computer monitor, feelings of indifference, frustration, lack of appreciation, depression, guilt, feeling fearful, paranoia that leads to avoiding computers and negative attitudes.

A further influence may be job insecurity and job uncertainty with regard to changing roles in the workplace, professional jealousy, and demotivation.

## Types of Technostress

There are five types of technostress that are found in the literature:

**Techno-overload:** Introduction of technology requires people to work faster and faster

**Techno-invasion:** Workers describe being "always exposed" to the extent that they can be reached anywhere and everywhere, and it is impossible to "cut away." This got even worse during the Covid era, with the growth of telecommuting. This may also go hand in hand with techno-isolation, which are psychological and social symptoms related to being cut off from the office environment, and resulting lack of workplace camaraderie and socialization, with resulting effects on workplace engagement.

**Techno Complexity:** These are situations where people spend time and effort to learn new technology, software and applications. People may find this activity intimidating, leading to stress.

**Techno-insecurity** is when people feel stressed about losing their jobs to other people more able to understand new gadgets and software.

**Techno-uncertainty** is driven by the short life span of computer systems. The average version of Microsoft Windows is about two years. Windows 10, which was introduced in 2020, is no longer be supported after July 2023. Computers that have this version of windows will gradually get slower and more vulnerable to cyber-attack. As a result, people are going to be faced with potential compatibility issues.

This is why people want to throw their computer out the window about half the time.

## Effects of Technostress on Employees

I suppose it goes without saying that if someone is in a constant battle with some sort of overaged PC or MRP system, there are going to be consequences. These include decreased job satisfaction, decreasing productivity, increased absenteeism and turnover rates, burnout and behavioral impacts.

In other words, just like introduction of technology into the workplace helped processes in some ways, it also increased some of the factors we have talked about relative to people not doing their jobs. People are ticked off, disengaged, unmotivated, and get into bad habits.

## Acceleration Effects

I am ready to say that technology works as an accelerant. On the good side, it enables improved productivity, improved alarm systems and reporting, and allows you to reach new markets at little or no cost.

But if you have workplace divisions, cultural issues, silos, and all of the other things that make organizations crazy, it will make that much worse too.

Example: In my observation, peoples' attitudes to technology depend on the level of technology available when the person was high school age. Social media use among the generation we now call "Generation Z" is much different than Millennials, who did not have that technology in high school.

Even worse is the boss, if he or she is still a "Boomer" it is likely he or she entered the workforce before the invention of the PC and cellphone. So, with a few exceptions the differences between these groups in the workforce regarding use of technology is made worse.

Social barriers will be exaggerated among these groups. There will be eye rolling and lack of teamwork.

## Superheroism Accelerated

In some workplaces, such as small businesses, superheroes emerge. We talked about them awhile back. Their proficiency with all sorts of tools, including technology, is so good that they start to do the work of the people around them.

Can you see where that is a danger? It is particularly dangerous when a company's trade secrets, customer lists, and other intellectual property can be packed out of the place on a thumb drive.

Also, the Superhero becomes a center of organizational authority that might fly in the face of the normal hierarchy, with resulting problem of people having multiple bosses, and lack of alignment in the work group.

## Work Shifting

Technology is a way to shift work from one group of people to another. The most obvious example of the checkout systems at Walmart. What happened? "They", as in "the Amorphous They" decided that Wally Mart could shift some of the work from themselves to us, the customers, and fire a lot of their cashiers. They have developed this self-scan system to do exactly that.

It represents a cost and effort reduction for them, but as we were saying, it is more work for us. We, the customers, are doing the work some low wage worker used to do.

There was a time, and there are still places, where your gas was pumped by a human. The automated gas pumps have shifted that cost to "us" too.

The invention of the PC shifted the work of what used to be called a "secretary" to the people who used to "need" them, mainly managers. In this era, having an "administrative assistant" is a sign of high status. That person's main job is to help some official manage their time and keep people out of their hair.

Did all of this cause technostress? Of course, it did, and we're all still trying to navigate all of this.

## Cultural Differences Accelerated

I go into workplaces all the time which are multicultural, and a substantial fraction of the workforce comes from less technologically advanced places. Whatever issues happen in the workplace anyway, it is accelerated even more by technology.

That includes cliques, informal communications, intergroup rivalries and other negative aspects of workforce organization

## Managing Technostress

Managing organizational technology is a serious challenge for some people. In some organizations, the IT infrastructure is literally the backbone of the business.

In this era, a substantial fraction of the value of the business is the ability to schedule jobs, track inventory, get process information, and use electronic data interchange with suppliers and customers to manage orders.

So, a conscious effort on the part of management is required to establish, maintain, and keep the system current. What that means is a significant expense in IT resources.

Managers will whine about this. They will say "All of our computers are on Windows XP. We can't possibly afford to change them out at once." What they're forgetting is that before computers, there was a room full of administrative assistants doing the work that is now done by the individual employees using these important tools.

## Information Transfer

There are a couple of places in the organization that are implementing work flow software. One of these is "customer relationship management" software, like Salesforce, and there is also something called CMMS or centralized maintenance management. Both of these do exactly the same thing: They take information that used to be kept in some experienced employee's brain, and transfer it to some way that it can become part of the organizational knowledge of the company.

In the case of the CRM software, it takes sales contacts, correspondence, and other background information and captures it in a system that enables following up of sales leads. It also is a critical element in the negotiation process in some places. It can be used to capture the effectiveness of promotional activities as well.

It also allows you to fire your senior sales people, because you have the status of all of his or her sales leads captured so that some other person can follow up on it.

In the case of maintenance management, it captures which pieces of equipment in a place break down, or require preventive maintenance, and allows that to be systematized as well.

What do these things have in common? These things used to be done by a manager, who retained all of this wisdom for himself. It also requires the sales people and maintenance people in an organization, who tend to be male and a bit hard headed, to follow discipline during the input process to avoid this turning into garbage.

Is this technostressful for them? Of course. Because of their personalities, these two groups tend to be the least cooperative when it comes to sitting down and entering anything into any database.

Managing change is what we are talking about. These people also dislike change.

## Artificial Intelligence

This is a huge can of worms. Artificial intelligence is being more and more widely used for daily functions.

Let's ask it for suggestions on how we are supposed to manage it. Here is a link for my chat:

Chat GPT Script

https://chat.openai.com/share/c6f20efa-a98a-475f-8cf1-f3509243e943

**Me:** Can you give me some suggestions from a psychological point of view on how to encourage the slow-adopters to this technology?

**Chat GPT:** Certainly! Encouraging slow-adopters to embrace new technology, including AI, often involves a combination of psychological and practical strategies. Here are some suggestions:

Education and Training:

Offer comprehensive training programs that cater to different learning styles. Address the psychological barriers by providing hands-on experiences and gradual exposure to the technology. This helps build confidence and familiarity.

Demonstrate Value:

Clearly communicate the tangible benefits of using the technology. Illustrate how it can enhance productivity, streamline tasks, and contribute to personal and professional growth. Understanding the value can motivate individuals to overcome their reservations.

User-Friendly Design:

Ensure that the AI tools are user-friendly and intuitive. A design that prioritizes ease of use can significantly reduce anxiety and frustration among users. A positive initial experience can foster a more receptive attitude toward the technology.

Support and Resources:

Provide ongoing support and resources for users. Establish accessible help desks, tutorials, and forums where individuals can seek assistance. Feeling supported in the learning process can ease psychological resistance.

Incorporate User Feedback:

Actively seek and incorporate feedback from users. This not only empowers individuals by making them feel heard but also allows for continuous improvement of the technology based on user preferences and needs.

Gradual Implementation:

Introduce the technology gradually rather than implementing it all at once. This phased approach allows individuals to acclimate to the changes at a comfortable pace, reducing the psychological impact of abrupt shifts.

Address Personalization:

Highlight how the technology can be personalized to suit individual preferences and work styles. This level of customization can make the technology feel more adaptable to individual needs, fostering a sense of control.

Peer Support and Mentoring:

Encourage a sense of community by fostering peer support networks or mentoring programs. Having colleagues who have successfully adopted the technology share their experiences and tips can be reassuring and motivating.

Celebrate Successes:

Acknowledge and celebrate individual and team successes related to the use of technology. Positive reinforcement can create a more positive attitude and a willingness to explore additional features and functionalities.

Emphasize Lifelong Learning:

Cultivate a culture of lifelong learning within the organization. Emphasize that the adoption of new technology is part of an ongoing process of skill development and adaptation, promoting a growth mindset.

By addressing the psychological aspects of technology adoption and implementing these strategies, you can create a more supportive and encouraging environment for slow-adopters, helping them transition more comfortably into the use of new technologies.

**Me:** Very good. Can you give me a few references from which I can draw for more information?

(I have posted the entire script in the Links and References)

It's actually fairly impressive. Better get used to it. Also, better get used to the embedding of a QR code into books, so that you can easily access online resources.

## Is that it?

No, that is not it. Managing technology has become an enormously important activity, and yet another realm in which people don't do their jobs.

It is subject to the same rules of human behavior: Impairment, lack of respect for rules, employee underdevelopment, employee personality issues and lack of defined work instructions.

It is also true to say that a new type of incompetence, IT incompetence, has become a new element of failure. It will be up to some future management to deal with this and act accordingly.

In any of the above cases, it's a management and resource function and ultimately, if there is technostress, it's the management's responsibility to sort it out if they can.

Links and References

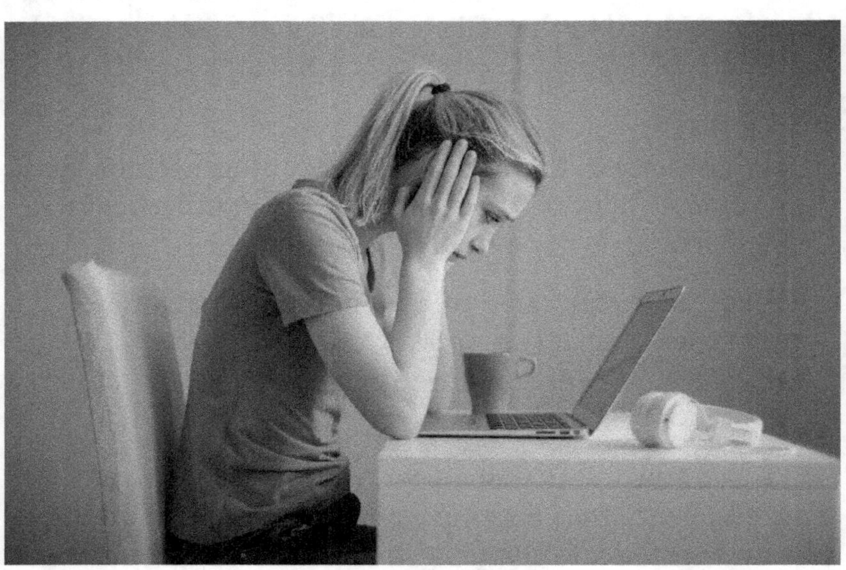

# 17 Consultants

We're now going to examine the topic of consultants. Consultants are in roughly the same category as Temps and Outsourcing, but are more often brought into an organization on a contract basis to provide something less tangible than fighting an oil fire or fixing a railroad derailment.

It's to provide wisdom and various other forms of advice. The output is "intellectual."

## Nicolo Machiavelli (1469-1527)

We're going to re-invoke this fellow.

Nicolo Machiavelli is one of the patron saints of Consulting. He was born into an influential family in Florence. He began as a diplomat in the days of the Italian city-states, and therefore made the acquaintance of the local bigwigs and the Church.

https://youtu.be/9_bo9X4B_eQ

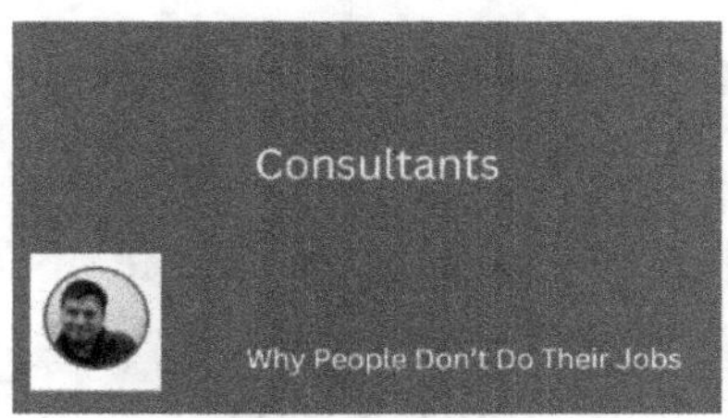


This is one of the most interesting periods in history in terms of social and political development. There was intrigue, betrayal, cooperation, and a lot of other gamesmanship among the nobility of the era.

At one point in 1513 he was accused of treachery, and spent three weeks being tortured by the Medici. After his release, he retired to his estate, which he had one of, and began his writing career in the topics of history and politics. He also had a nice side gig representing the Florentine Republic in Italy, Germany and France, and rather than engage directly in politics, he chose a less risky path of writing and studying. He began to understand a lot about human nature.

He became an expert in defining and capturing the political histories of Rome and Greece, and explored the balance between what is now called "idealism" and "pragmatism" and in any sort of leadership or management capacity the reality of shifting back and forth between these two ideals.

His name is now associated with deceit, treachery and crime. But, behind that there was an underlying respect for humanity, and paved the way for modern "republicanism", which is a term that means that the people get to decide things.

"The Prince" which is his most famous work, talks a lot about management balancing these two things for the overall good of the organization, or kingdom, as the case may be. At some point he derived a revenue source from riding around and giving management advice to the rulers of the day.

## Consultant History

Consulting is actually a lot older than that. There have always been sources of wisdom in an organization, as far back as the hunters and gatherers. These people had a special name: "Grandparents." The tribe or social organization fed them, and kept them around because they were a source of "organizational knowledge." They had made all of the screw-ups possible and knew where the skeletons were buried, sometimes literally.

In the business world, there was once a practice of keeping old timers around. In the place where I worked, there was an old guy named Lyle that was actually younger than I am now. His job was to come in every day and not change anything. He unlocked a big safe, full of proprietary formulas, opened them up in front of him on the desk, and lit up a cigarette, which was common in those days, and stared off into space for a few hours.

His job was to manage the formulas. Any changes, other than very minor in the formulations might have had effects in the field, but "tweaks" were allowed, and if needed he did that. He came in with the first load of bricks in 1947, and knew every screw-up that had happened, and what the cause was.

"They" kept him around because he had that role. He was a tribal elder.

## The Modern Theory about Organizational Knowledge

At some time in the 1980's this whole idea was turned on its head. There was consolidation in every industry. This was partly because of the invention and widespread use of the PC, and corporate takeover activity that happened in that time period. Tribal elders were considered a luxury.

The company I was with at the time was bought out 4 times in 8 years. As it was explained to me, "if you knew what you were doing you would not have been bought out."

At that point, use of consultants became much more widespread. There were a few instances that I knew of in which people that were downsized were immediately rehired by their organizations because, little did anyone know, they really did know what they were doing.

## Not Anyone Could Do This

I have to say this as well. Our guy Lyle would not have been an especially good consultant. He had a very detailed historical perspective of one tiny operation. The people that had better luck being consultants were those with higher level knowledge of systems and processes, and detailed technical knowledge of specific projects that could be applied on a more widespread basis.

Office Space—The Two Bobs

https://youtu.be/RkmuI5W694o?si=KCO1qAKdL_zBHoMt

In this example, the "Two Bobs" have high level systems knowledge in software development, and are probing around an organization prior to some kind of feared reorganization.

That brings us basically to the modern era.

## Appropriate uses of Consultants

Here are some uses and misuses of consultants, based on my experience of being one, and being around several.

| Use | Description |
|---|---|
| Bringing in expertise that is not available currently | Allows the organization to take advantage of expertise when and where it was needed |
| Shorten the learning | Undertake projects knowing where the main areas of concern are |

| curve | |
|---|---|
| Take advantage of personal relationships | In a sales function, gain access to customers and decision makers in a target business, usually a customer. |
| Provide "Fresh Eyes." | Evaluate current methods and systems as a way to initiate business improvements |

| **Misuse** | **Description** |
|---|---|
| Validating decisions that are already made | Hired "Yes Man" |
| Giving the Boss's crony a few extra paychecks | Done for various reasons |
| Shifting the blame for some hard decision to someone external | Allows management to say "the consultants told us to do that." |
| Deliberate failure | Allows the boss to say "We tried. Now let's |

| | |
|---|---|
| | do it my way." |

## Cautions on the Use of Consultants

There are a couple of things that are interesting on this.

## It Ticks off Current Employees

First of all, hiring a consultant is sort of an admission that the current employees don't know what they are doing, and has a tendency to tick them off.

I have been in meetings a dozen times, particularly in a product development setting, where there is disagreement on an idea. There are usually two factions, a "full speed ahead" faction, and a "fearful" faction. Or, if you are one of the "fearful" people you might say it's a "crazy" faction and a "slow and steady wins the race" faction.

Anyway, you get the dynamic.

In either case, there are people in the room who have the right answer but no one will listen to them. But the consultant makes a suggestion, the groupthink sets in, and someone in the corner says "yeah I told you that a year ago."

## There are Potential Legal Issues

There are some cans of worms here regarding use of a consultant to try to discover trade secrets. Some of these consultants have non-compete agreements, and other agreements that may result in a lawsuit.

Also, consultants may give advice that is illegal in a given jurisdiction. If that is the case, there may be financial damages, and liability.

In either case, the consultants themselves often have no skin in the game.

## They Represent "Top Down" Problem Solving

This is also an issue, and it causes more resentment among the lower levels of the organization. A consultant comes in and makes a pronouncement and throws it over the cubicle wall into the organization that has to implement it.

This causes lack of ownership of the project on the basis of the organization, and resultant implementation is weaker anyway.

## Thought Question:

Say, for example, you're in an organization with employees that are ticked off, impaired disengaged and undertrained. Your facilities are insufficient, your customer base is shrinking, and your management and supervision is indifferent and annoying.

Is there any consultant in the world that can come in and fix it, other than TV?

## TV Consultants

I sort of like these shows, because they go through a lot of the thought processes that you, yourself, could very well go through if you were solving a problem in your business.

Here's a list.

| **Show** | **Network** | **Description** |
|---|---|---|
| Bar Rescue | Para-mount | Loud mouthed consultant turns around a failing bar by using actual hospitality management techniques |
| Homestead Rescue | Discovery | Family of homesteaders from Alaska try to turn around homesteads run by people who have no business doing it. |
| Kitchen Nightmares | Fox | Famous chef comes into family run businesses to improve the menu and service. |
| Hotel Impossible | Travel Channel | Ex-manager of fancy hotel tries to improve run down hotels and motels in resort areas. |
| Tabatha's Salon Takeover | Bravo | Snooty high end beauty salon operator tries to turn around a failing beauty salon. |
| The Profit | NBC | Famous business person |

| | | |
|---|---|---|
| | | buys part of a failing business and using management improvement methods turns it around (usually.) |

## These are all basically the Same Show

These shows are considered "semi-reality" in that the "rescues" are formulaic, and the producers select cases that are particularly interesting from a drama point of view.

They love people standing around in a business screaming at each other, or bursting into tears.

There is an entrenched, mediocre manager or owner, very often in a family business. The "consultant" appears on the scene, makes an assessment, of some appalling nature. There is some data analysis, or other analysis, to determine the extent of the problems.

Very often, the show producers drop some expensive piece of equipment or infrastructure into the place, in cases where the management couldn't otherwise afford them. In a few of these, there's a makeover, including decor, branding, and store layout.

At the same time, there is an examination of the people involved. There is usually one or more disengaged, ticked off, impaired employees with mental health issues that needs to be fired. Very often, the boss him or herself is part of the problem for failing to accept the reality of the situation, or bear the cost of change.

Behind the scenes there is a crew that works frantically to make these changes based on some artificially imposed time deadline.

At the end of it, there is a big reveal, and/or party with a lot of "before and after", and some tearful farewells, usually. Some of the cases revert right back to old habits rather than make the needed changes. Sometimes it's "good riddance."

Does this work? The Bar Rescue success rate at this point is said to be about 50% based on people who have made it their business to find this out.  Based on this limited sample, this may be about right. Some people have no business running businesses, as we have already found out.

## The Consultant Acceptance Curve

As someone who has worked as a consultant, I am going to run a graph by you:

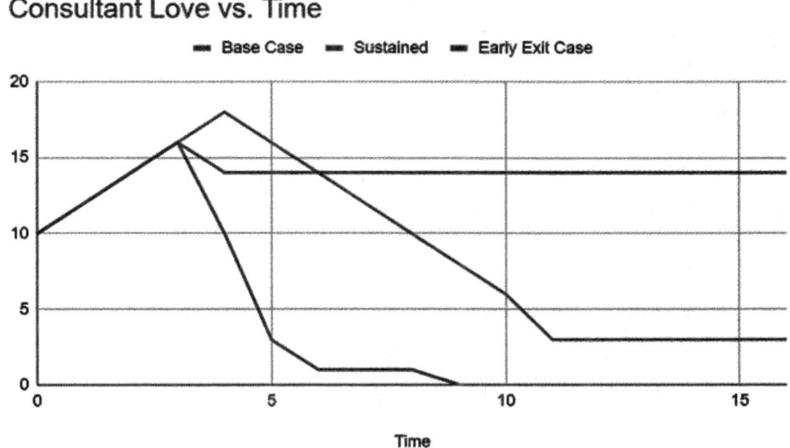

Along the X axis, we have time. This can be any time units you wish to think about. I am only interested in the shapes of the curves.

On the Y axis is "Consultant Love" from the point of view of the client. "Love Units" are any units of affection you care to substitute.

The base case is the top line, above. Let's say, that when a consultant is first hired, the love level is a "10". As time goes on, the consultant contributes wisdom and does something useful, and the level of love on the part of the client increases.

There is some maximum point, after which the consultant's act becomes worn out and there is a steady decline in love, to the point where the consultant is not valued in the organization as much as on the first day. This may be due to factions within the business back biting each other. This may be due to the consultant not contributing as much. In some projects this happens when the main goal of the project is accomplished.

The biblical proverb "A prophet in his own land is without honor" applies in this case. The consultant has jumped the shark.

The bottom line is where this happens right away, the consultant's value goes to zero, and the client tells him or her to get lost.

What the consultant hopes for sometimes is the middle case, where the consultant delivers excellent work and this goes on for a long time. Sometimes, however, the consultant is perfectly content to let the organization sink or swim on its own.

## Consultant Hiring Strategy

None of these are considered "bad." What is more accurate to say is that sometimes it's the nature of the job for the consultant to deliver his wisdom and get lost. Sometimes, it's the nature of the job for the consultant to be around for a while to be more nurturing.

It is desirable for "the organization" and the consultant to give this some thought, and structure the agreement to have a finite life span. The best consulting job I had was exactly like that. It was 90 days, we all parted as friends, and the client got what they needed.

What neither party wants is a consulting relationship where the client is tempted to sick guard dogs or rub the desk down with ammonia to get rid of him or her, because that causes resentment, and is unproductive.

I have seen some of these curves in reality, from both sides, and the consultant staying too long does no one any good.

## Consultants Doing Their Job

Here is my general opinion on this topic:

As long as the job is clearly defined, the deliverables are openly stated, and both parties are in agreement on the implementation, consultants are fine. The consultant will do his or her job and both parties will benefit

In fact, if you clearly define the job and deliverables, and everyone is in agreement on implementation, regular employees are fine. Employees will do their jobs.

Consultants in the real world are no magic solution for anything.

Links and References

# 18 Unknownership

I'm going to spend a little time on this topic, because it has grown into the forefront in the last year or two.

"Unknownership" is a significant demotivator, and contributing cause of people not doing their jobs.

Unknownership is where there is a disconnect between the ownership of the company and the regular employees.

In a family business, or in a startup, people know who is in charge and running the place. Also, if the manager is good, there is a coherent corporate strategic direction, and people are motivated sometimes by a "cause."

When a company gets too big, and its stock starts to be traded in index funds, "Unknownership" kicks in.

https://youtu.be/mKHHARAL12o

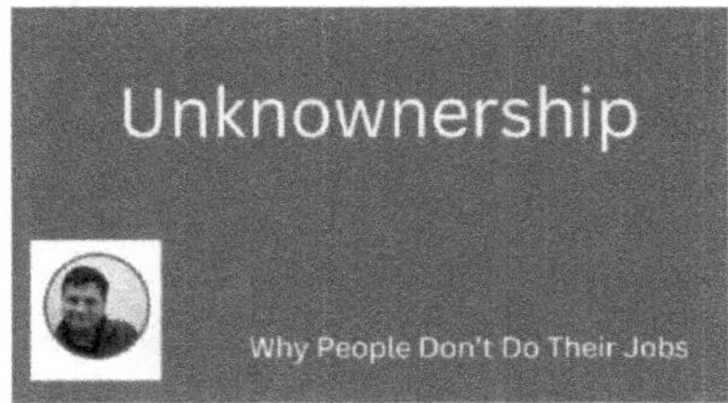

## Unknownership Example

We're going to look at the Norfolk Southern Railroad now. In the above video we were focused on Lockheed and Boeing, but it all comes to about the same.

One of their trains wrecked recently, and nearly blew up a little town in Ohio, because a series of people didn't do their jobs.

Here are the top 10 shareholders of that company. "Institutional Investors" own 76 percent of the company:

| Holder | Shares | Date Reported | % Out |
|---|---|---|---|
| Vanguard Group Inc | 18.5M | Sep 30, 2023 | 8.18% |
| Blackrock Inc. | 15.31M | Sep 30, 2023 | 6.77% |
| JP Morgan Chase & Company | 12.8M | Sep 30, 2023 | 5.66% |
| State Street Corporation | 9.02M | Sep 30, 2023 | 3.99% |
| Lazard Asset Management LLC | 8.63M | Sep 30, 2023 | 3.82% |
| Dodge & Cox Inc | 6.42M | Sep 30, 2023 | 2.84% |
| Price (T.Rowe) Associates Inc | 5.76M | Sep 30, 2023 | 2.55% |
| Geode Capital Management, LLC | 4.26M | Sep 30, 2023 | 1.89% |
| Wells Fargo & Company | 4.19M | Sep 30, 2023 | 1.85% |
| Capital World Investors | 3.61M | Sep 30, 2023 | 1.60% |

Here is a list of the major shareholders of CSX corporation, which is another railroad that covers more or less the same part of the country:

| Holder | Shares | Date Reported | % Out |
|---|---|---|---|
| Vanguard Group Inc | 176.53M | Sep 30, 2023 | 8.93% |
| Blackrock Inc. | 142.35M | Sep 30, 2023 | 7.20% |
| State Street Corporation | 83.34M | Sep 30, 2023 | 4.22% |
| Capital World Investors | 65.41M | Sep 30, 2023 | 3.31% |
| Price (T.Rowe) Associates Inc | 54.89M | Sep 30, 2023 | 2.78% |
| Soroban Capital Partners LP | 42.82M | Sep 30, 2023 | 2.16% |
| Geode Capital Management, LLC | 39.06M | Sep 30, 2023 | 1.98% |
| Capital International Investors | 35.31M | Sep 30, 2023 | 1.79% |
| Bank of America Corporation | 31.04M | Sep 30, 2023 | 1.57% |
| Lazard Asset Management LLC | 29.19M | Sep 30, 2023 | 1.48% |

As you can see, there is an overlap. Five of the top 10 institutional shareholders in both of these companies is the same. The reason for this is not necessarily nefarious. These railroads are big, and Vanguard and Blackrock are running "index funds" that are required to invest in these big, exchange traded companies.

The "index funds" are very popular among pension plans, insurance companies, and the like. If you have a 401K investing in an index fund, you are a participant in this system.

The companies themselves are run by the CEO, but the CEO is chosen by the Board of Directors. Let's see what kind of qualifications we have on the boards of these two companies.

| **Norfolk Southern** | **CSX Corporation** |
|---|---|
| Real Estate | Publishing |
| College President | Bioengineering |
| Military | Construction |
| Fast Food | "Capital Management" |
| Accounting | Current CEO |
| Software | Banking |
| Aerospace | Banking |
| Banking | Military/IT |
| Mining | Steel |
| Manufacturing | Mining |
| Movie Theaters | Chemicals |
| Railroad | |
| Scientific Testing | |
| Current CEO | |

The funny thing about these two lists is that they are too perfect. A couple of bankers, a couple of retail people, a couple of "capital management" people. I will let you go through and figure out the racial and gender balance. I know a TV script when I see it. All that is missing is them being stranded on a life raft, or on an island somewhere.

I also have to say that being on the board of directors of companies looks a pretty good gig, if you can get it. A lot of these people are on the boards of several organizations. That is a way to reward someone for being that kind of person. They live in places like South Florida, and Virginia Beach VA, and Northern California. They've all been to the same business schools.

The Norfolk Southern website has a PDF that I have linked that summarizes the "expertise" of their board of directors. They seem to think a lot of the qualifications of their CEO, who, according to them is gifted in everything. The board has three things in common: They've all had experience being CEO, they've all had experience on Boards of Directors, and they all are "expert" in "Strategic planning."

## You can see what happens

With a couple of exceptions these companies are run by basically the same group of people, who rotate on and off the boards of directors, rotate in and out of CEO positions. They know each other. It makes sense. From the point of view of the mutual fund managers, you want to entrust that much money to people you know.

Does that, in and of itself, prevent people from doing their jobs? No, not really, but if you go back to the chapter on organizational development, you will see the possibility that these people are all in a bubble. There is limited flow of information in and out of the bubble. They live in the same places and do strategic planning together, as that fellow F. Scott Fitzgerald, who knew all about the bubble, might say.

They all plan the same way, and have the same inside language, because they all had the same professors. I'll bet they don't even know what "Unknownership" is.

That is the very definition of entrenchment. The CEOs of these places tend to promote "bubble people" into the upper-level management. These are also the same people that can't relate to alarm systems, can't possibly understand the low wage workers, and have completely different reward systems. They are rewarded by the mutual fund managers for doing their job, which is to maximize the wealth of the shareholders.

There is evidence which I have posted in the links that says that they're not even especially smart. But they are good at staying in the bubble.

## The System Sort of Works

This system sort of works. This group of "strategic planners" can keep things running fairly reasonably. They can allocate their capital expenditures, they can do mergers and acquisitions, and stock buybacks and run the financial aspects of their businesses. If things get tough, and their decisions underperform, there is someone else from the bubble to substitute.

But at some point, there is an excellent chance for them to lose engagement. Do you remember the chapter on startups? Well, this is how aggressive self-starters get bored and start their own company.

This is why decisions like we saw in some of the previous chapters got made. This is why the corporate middle managers and QC inspectors become disengaged, at roughly the same rate as the low wage workers. This is why the nicest public rest room in the world is at IHG headquarters, and not in the Holiday Inn in Erlanger KY. This is why, when you try to call a human, the human doesn't know. This is why there is a vast, untrained, impaired, ticked off workforce.

This system could go on for a long time just as it is. But there are times of discontinuous change, where "strategic planning" doesn't work anymore. It had been a long time since something really screwed up has happened, until Covid hit, and I am afraid that Covid was just a warmup for the real tests that are ahead of us.

Can the "bubble people" adapt? I don't know. But, as we have said several times, a system is perfectly designed to produce what it does. We have a workforce where 75% of the employees have "quiet quit," some huge fraction of them is sick, drunk and sleep deprived, and stuck in low wage jobs permanently. And, people don't do their jobs in unprecedented numbers.

If we ever had to start producing tanks and jeeps again, in a hurry, we wouldn't be able to do it. Strategic Planning has its limits, but right now it pays better. At some point we're going to need implementers.

Links and References

# 19 Denial and Resistance

We're going to talk about human emotion now, in this case it's the two emotions of Denial and Resistance, which are very powerful ways in which people don't do their jobs.

In this case, the people we're talking about would be "management" as defined somehow. Let's say that we're not talking about the people in the bubble, although this certainly applies to some of them. We're talking about the people that are ultimately responsible for people doing their jobs, and providing resources and systems that allow them to do so.

Before we talk about that, we're going to talk about management failure.

https://youtu.be/D21fHO4VZbA

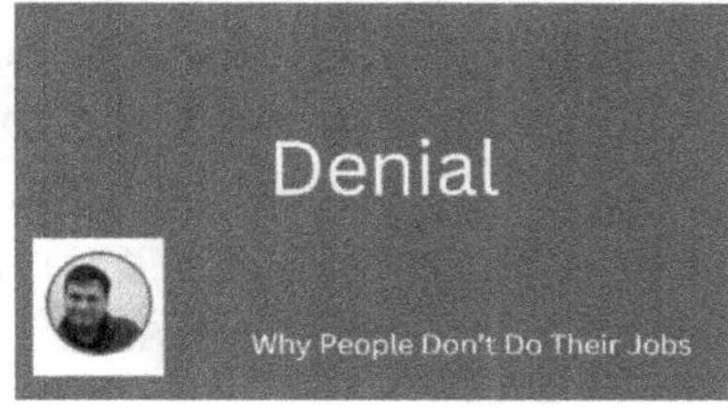

## Management Failure Modes

The ISO standard that I work with all the time, if read a certain way, is a list of possible ways that a management can screw up. This being the case it makes sense to walk through a few of these. There is a point to all of this, as you will see when we get to the end.

We can have fun with this, if we want. We can pretend we're the writers of a little sitcom about life in the factory. There are characters and products, and funny things that happen. Except, of course, that most of the time it's not funny.

Let's envision this little factory. Or, it can be a big factory. Or, it can be a pizza place if we want it to be. It doesn't really matter.

It is run by a manager of some kind, and there is a crew, and products. It can be a service too, but for the moment, products are easier for some of us to get our brains around.

## Being Blindsided by External Events

Here's the first one. There's a knock on the door, and someone is going to make life miserable for our poor company.

In this failure mode, everything is going along fine, until it isn't and it is unanticipated. Here are some examples: The strip shop the business is in about to be torn down. The little company is across the street from an Amazon distribution center that pays $2 more an hour than they do. A key employee, a superhero, walks off the job.

Most of these things are externally derived, but the management doesn't anticipate them, and has no plan to deal with them when they happen.

We won't even talk about Covid for the moment

## Not being Committed to the Business

This one happens quite often. If someone asks the manager why he or she is in the business, they can't come up with a reason, other than to make money. That means they have no longer term goal for the business, no plan to expand into other markets, or change with conditions or anything else.

Quite often the business rationale is to ultimately turn the whole thing over to the kids, in the case of a family business, or to skip out and head to the beach. Lack of a strategic direction basically means that the management is disengaged, and that flows downward into the organization.

Not being committed to the customers is slightly worse, by the way. Sometimes, these entrenched, mediocre managers consider customers a nuisance.

The responsibility of management is to increase the wealth of the shareholders, but it is also important for there to be some sort of desire to benefit society somehow. If a company doesn't want to benefit society, then what's the point?

## Fundamentally Flawed Business Planning

I think we referred to this earlier on, but let me give you an example. A pizza, at a pizza place, sells for about $20 right now. Of that, the cost is about ⅔ or roughly $14. A business owner, or manager, should therefore know exactly how many pizzas that he or she needs to sell to pay his or her $1000 a month rent, and pay him or herself a little salary while they are making people happy with their pizza.

You would be shocked at how many managers aren't able to do this simple math problem, and don't make appropriate decisions to bring in traffic.

The same thing works on a much bigger scale in the case of manufacturing. Part of the issue with startups is unrealistic estimates of what things cost. What the production costs are, and what the selling price is going to be. If there is a fundamental shift in conditions, the assumptions that were true at the start of the project are no longer true.

Do you want an example of this? The average life span of an automotive assembly plant is 20 years. That's less than the working life span of a young employee that starts when the plant does. Sometime in that 20-year period, something happened. Economics changed, automobile styles changed, or some other change happened that cause the plant to be no longer viable.

Do you know what's worse than shutting down? The hostage crisis that happens beforehand. The plant manager calls everybody in and says "we're the high-cost plant now. We're going to have to cut your pay, or make you work more. If you don't give us these concessions, the plant will shut down." They hold the local government hostage. "Build us a new rail line or the plant will shut down, and all of these people will be out of work."

The city, or county, rolls over and gives up some kickbacks or other concessions and 18 months later, the whole thing happens again.

## Lack of Metrics

Sorry that business has a lot of math in it, but the really good managers use it to understand how they're doing.

Most companies, of any size, have different measurements so that they can tell how their business processes are running. This allows them to answer the simple question, "is your business successful?"

The best one is sales dollars, or profits. Most of the time, a manager knows what the monthly sales are, and can make adjustments to their marketing efforts if need be. A manager of a department in a giant factory is fed these all the time, through some dashboard or some other process.

That way, there's an early predictor of some problem with the business, such as people not doing their jobs, that can be fixed before the whole thing goes under.

## Poor or Nonexistent Change Control

We saw an example of that awhile back with the airbag company. Takata found out they needed to move production to Mexico and did so without validating the process.

A professionally run organization with alert management has a process by which if something changes, particularly anything that involves customers, it is done in a controlled way with a lot of communication.

## Resources are Insufficient

This one is common, if not universal. By "resources" we're talking about what the employees need to run the business. This would be manpower (or person power) infrastructure, environment, and measurement resources.

How do you know whether a business has enough resources? Well, if it is meeting its metrics, and making people happy with its products or services, then that is an indicator.

But if the boss is cheap, and not committed to the business, this is where it will show up.

In the corporate environment, there is a process by which, if resources are needed, and there is a justifiable business case to be made, there is an obligation on the part of management to provide them, or rethink their commitment to the business.

IT infrastructure is no exception. If the boss is so cheap that the computers in the place are still running Windows 7, and the MRP system hasn't had an upgrade in more than a decade, it's a sign that the boss isn't doing his or her job.

## HR Policies and Training are Inadequate

We had a whole chapter on training a while back. A lot of people are just thrown out onto the line, and don't get training at all. There may be on -the-job training from someone that is just as new as they are. There are no refreshers. If anything changes, there is no thoughtful policy on retraining.

I am invoking McCaig's Law, and saying that if a company has high turnover, hiring processes are not effective, there are lawsuits, and the workforce has no training program, it's going to be a chaotic organization. People aren't doing their jobs.

## Order Review and Acceptance

This is a common failure mode. The customer calls and says "Can you have it here by Thursday" and it doesn't get there by Thursday. People over-promise and under-deliver. Companies promote themselves as one thing, and come to find out, they are another thing.

If there is a catalog, or a menu, half of the things on it can't be done. Commitments are made and not followed. No one takes the time to find out what the customer really wants.

This really aggravates the customers, because back in the beginning of all of this, there should have been some kind of customer commitment.

There is a change process here too. Someone calls up and says "you know I said I wanted it red, but I've changed my mind and now I want it green" there has to be a process to communicate that to the production process so that everyone is on the same page.

## Product Underdevelopment

We saw a couple of examples of product development failure earlier. Do you want another example? The electric cars that run out of juice too soon. The marketing people say "We need a 100-mile recharge distance." The R and D people say "no problem, we'll just use the super-expensive batteries we were working with," The marketing people say "you can't do that. It'll push the price of the car too high. Our competitors will kill us." And then the R and D people say "Sorry, it's physics."

So, a lot of these get into the marketplace and customers are annoyed because the 100-mile recharge becomes a 75-mile recharge, and a lot of people run out of power in the middle of nowhere. That's because the marketing people put out a lot of press releases and product brochures that say 100 miles.

The two main failure modes are, failure to understand what the customers need in the first place, and then, running into some constraints somewhere in the development process and taking shortcuts.

The third problem, if there is one, is keeping track of changes. In the electric car model, this is where down in the bowels of the R and D department they OK the use of the cheaper batteries, but no one goes back upstream to tell the marketing department to update their product information. The marketing people are going around and saying one thing, and the R and D people are saying another thing.

## Recap

At this point we have almost enough elements in the business at this point to be able to write a little script of failure.

An organization is working with obsolete equipment. The boss is indifferent, because he or she is ready to sell it all and head to the beach. The equipment is breaking down. There is high turnover, nobody gets trained, infrastructure and facilities are terrible, and the rest rooms are a mess. Work instructions, if there are any, are written on sticky notes.

The Marketing department promises one thing, and the R and D department promises another thing, and nobody keeps records of anything, so there are constant customer complaints, and finger pointing.

The employees themselves are ticked off, show up drunk or high, under-educated low wage workers, and there are constant workplace anger issues. People walk in the door with tears streaming down their faces.

The sum total of this so far is that people aren't doing their jobs. This has some elements of a sitcom already. Except, it's not actually funny. It can be tragic.

Now it's time for purchasing.

## Purchasing Failure Modes

There are several main failure modes in purchasing. This is a much bigger story in manufacturing than it is in the service business, but that's not to say it doesn't happen.

One is, the organization buys from unreliable suppliers who can't provide the materials or goods to be used in production. In other words, they do business with people like themselves, who don't spend money on equipment and infrastructure, and the R and D and marketing people don't talk to each other.

Stuff shows up and doesn't meet the specification, or shows up late. But, the purchasing manager says, "I'm getting a great price."

Another one is, the organization gets a good supplier, and one sunny day the supplier is bought out and/or closed down. Or, maybe they are on some other continent and something happens to disrupt the supply chain. What then? There are electric cars that need to be produced. How does a company vet its suppliers to make sure they are financially sound enough to produce a reliable supply?

The third one is that the supplier does fraud. "Such a deal I have for you on these replacement airbags" they say. What they don't say is that they are counterfeit knockoffs, and when installed in a car they don't work at all. That has been known to happen.

The fourth one is that communications processes within the supplier's company are terrible and/or they just lie. "We can get it to you by Thursday."

There's a fifth one. The purchasing people are disengaged from what is going on in the plant. A sales guy and I once had to call on a purchasing agent in Alabama. This was a former trusted plant employee who got a "big promotion" to purchasing agent. This fellow had "arrived" because he now got to be entertained, in the "three martini lunch" way. There are a lot of side stories on this. But to make a long story short this fellow could be influenced by a sales person who did a good job of entertaining.

He was suddenly fired at one point, and his replacement, who we knew from a previous job, put a stop to all entertaining. It seems this fellow had ordered three years' supply of paper bags which were sitting in the plant getting dirty.

A lot of this has been done away with due to the use of MRP systems which do a better job of calculating usage levels and inventory, so maybe this type of thing has gone away.

Oh, I have a sixth one. The purchasing and sales people are not knowledgeable, and don't know what the hell they are ordering. They order some lethal quantity of a Weapon of Mass Destruction and it shows up on the shipping dock where it is unloaded by an illiterate warehouse crew to handle and store. What could possibly go wrong?

## Operations Failure Modes

So now we're to the point where the product has to be produced, or the service has to be done. If we are writing a sitcom, here is where it gets funny. Or, serious, if you're writing one of those late-night drama shows.

The first problem is something we keep  calling "controlled conditions" where the product is produced according to some design, or in a certain way.

There is a system of work instructions or product specifications that could get screwed up. Someone changes the drawing and doesn't tell the guy running the machine, or the machine program doesn't get updated.

There are others:  Equipment obsolete, and breaking down, and no way to get spare parts.

A work group of funny trained employees. A grouchy supervisor. A drug-fueled burnout, a pretty girl, a queen bee, being chased around by a group of drones. One or two straight men for comedic balance.

There is a system of identification or serial numbers so that someone can tell which part is which, and when it was produced.  Product specifications, which are important to making sure that the item that is produced doesn't match what the marketing department is telling the customers.

These things are all written on sticky notes which blow all over the floor when the truck bay door ls lifted.

There is a comical inspector. Let's make him officious, but harmless. The workers spend a lot of time trying to sneak defective product behind his back into boxes.

There is an area in the plant where defective product is stored. This thing is a giant pyramid of possible plot lines, centering on mediocrity.

## Alarm Systems

We already talked about alarm system failure,

In most professionally run organizations, there are several.

It doesn't have to be a little buzzer at the end of the assembly line that goes off when there is a scrap part. But it can be.

The professionally run organizations have metrics. There is scrap rate, that we talked about. There are plenty of others. On time shipments. Machine up-time. Cost variances. There are any number of measurements that a professional manager would look at and say "something is wrong."

Secondly, there are customer complaints. The customers are taking the time to communicate with the organization, and the professional manager says "something is wrong."

I want to invent the alarm that sounds like a baby crying.

After all of this, now, we're ready to talk about Denial and Resistance.

## Denial

This is the first one, and it is very powerful.

Imagine that you are the founder of the business. You have worked hard, day and night, to establish this business and get customers. Your first production runs were difficult. You lost your first couple of customers but got others.

Years go by and it is better. You are successful. You proudly put your hand on the door handle when you walk in the place. You think you have a world class organization.

The reality is different. Your workforce is drunk, disengaged and/or ticked off, and undertrained. The phone is ringing off the hook with complaints (actually if your phones still have hooks it may be time to modernize your infrastructure). Your R and D and Marketing people are in constant screaming fights. The assembly line is down for a week waiting for a 50-cent sprocket because your knucklehead maintenance foreman didn't have a stash of spare parts.

The little buzzer at the end of the line is broken.

You get the plant financials for the month from your staff accountant who is a superhero, who has been circulating his or her resume for some time now.

The metrics are terrible. A third of your orders are delivered late. There are constant returns and complaints. What do you say?

"No, that can't be right, there must be some kind of mistake. I will just ignore this. This is a world class organization."

So, nothing gets changed, or fixed. You, the boss, are in denial.

Based on my experience, with hundreds of companies and dozens of startups across many industries, this is common. I have seen it many times. There is an obvious problem but management refuses to change it. That is one of the very definitions of entrenched mediocrity.

Sometimes they kill the messenger. They say "those metrics can't be right" and throw them into the trash, and fire the statistician. By the way, do you know another sign of this? The organization goes through QC inspectors about once a year. Quality control, the voice of the customer, gets less respect than production.

Sometimes, management is just out to lunch. They themselves are disengaged, and it is easier to deny the problem rather than do something about it.

## Signs of a Boss in Denial

There is an interesting article from Popular Science in which the statistic is given that 23% of CEOs were fired due to being in a state of denial.

What are they in denial about? Here is a table.

| Denial Topic | Comments |
|---|---|
| What their employees know. | Employees can tell, much better than a disengaged manager, how things are going. They know if orders are slow. They know if materials are bad. They know how much more efficient and |

| | |
|---|---|
| | better the place could be. |
| What their employees (or customers) want. | The most common of these is "I know I pay my employees well." There is lack of understanding of the local labor market. But sometimes, employees just want a little respect.<br><br>I was in a place once where the common management belief was "our customers don't care whether or not they get their stuff on time. It just goes into inventory." They make mistakes about customer perception and product acceptance all the time. |
| Their control over their department or company. | Steven Covey has this saying "strength is weakness, and weakness is strength." Controlling managers that think they are in control of everything are very often in control of nothing. There is a superhero or two in the background who may be running everything. |
| The degree to which their employees trust and respect | This is actually a good one. Many managers have a false perception of themselves as a leader. |

| | |
|---|---|
| them. | |
| Their own feelings of fear and powerless-ness. | This is also a good one, self-explanatory in light of the respect issue. A bad manager knows deep down that he or she is in trouble. |

I also linked an article about what happens when the boss is one of those people that embraces conspiracy theories. There are a lot of those people around right now, and they are very dangerous from a business standpoint, where facts and logic are important.

You only need to look at the poor "My Pillow" guy to see what happens when a boss goes off the deep end. How would you like to be a quality assurance person in that place?

## Denial and Alcoholism

There is a psychological link between this kind of behavior and alcoholism and other forms of addiction. It is quite likely that some of the "drive" that gets these people to be successful in the first place is a bit of an addictive tendency.

The first step of the 12-step program is to admit there is a problem.

It was well put, in the article I have linked:

*In the world of psychology, denial is typically understood as a defense mechanism. This means that people sometimes use denial (and other defense mechanisms) to avoid facing realities that are too stressful or painful to deal with.*

*-De Marais in Good RX*

There is a school of thought that someone working for a boss in denial should treat them in the same way as they would treat a drug addict or alcoholic.

Help is out there, like the 800-numbers say. There is no 800 number for reporting a boss who is in denial that I know of. Maybe I should start one, and offer the service of laying it out to him or her.

## Resistance

Resistance, with a capital R, is an invention of Stephen Pressfield, who is the award-winning author of "The Legend of Bagger Vance."

Resistance, as he puts it, is the universal force that keeps things the same.

He used it in the context of being a writer. Pressfield himself aspired to do novels and screenplays and that kind of thing, which is a noble cause. He is an interesting fellow.

Why People Still Don't Do Their Jobs

https://youtu.be/Fpm1VwyZng0

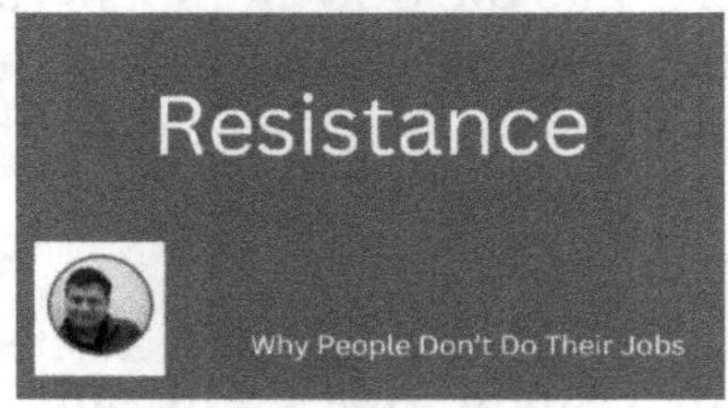


As he, himself, puts it, he spent 17 years trying to write, before he earned a penny, and 27 years before he got his first novel published.

He may be one of those cases we talked about before, where he was in the wrong job, some of which included driving trucks, working as an advertising copy writer, and picking fruit with the immigrants to make a few dollars while he refined his art.

At this point, he has become one of the members of the "self-improvement" community and will give you a free course on "The War of Art" in which he explains this concept to you.

To make a long story short, he says "Resistance" is 100% internal, but it has external allies. The number one symptom of "Resistance" is hesitation to do the work.

Resistance is the negative, self-sabotaging voice in your head that says "you can't".

Pressfield is "anthropomorphizing" this internal self-talk into some sort of living creature, like a monster, which has as its mission to keep the victim from doing what they must.

Resistance only works in one direction, the upward. There is no resistance for things getting worse. That's the concept we talked about earlier with regard to entropy. Entropy is the universal force that, unless otherwise acted on, will send an organization into decline.

I will leave this for the moment except to say this:

The reason that organizations (and people) don't get any better is because improving it is hard. Managers, especially when they get to a certain point, don't want to face the challenge anymore.

That's why known problems are not dealt with. Investments are not made. No effort is made to find out what is going on in the industry or neighborhood, and alarm systems are ignored or denied. It's work, and no one wants to do it because it is hard.

## Symptoms of Resistance

There is a list of things that are indicators that you are falling under the influence of Resistance. Distraction, procrastination, rationalization, getting into some kind of trouble, victimization. We all know people that from time to time slip into these ways of this type of thinking

All of these are examples of how Resistance is keeping them, or you from some higher state of being.

This is also the point at which bad habits sneak in, such as substance abuse.

In the extreme cases, Resistance can become clinical. It can lead to depression, aggression, or other types of dysfunctions.

## Ways to Deal with Resistance

The one and only way to deal with Resistance is to sit down and do the work.

The taking of one first step even if it is a failure is a defeat of Resistance.

The second step, if there is such a thing, is a concept called "turning pro" which is to say, do the things a professional would do in the field of endeavor that you are in.

This includes such things as asking for help, seeking a mentor, not accepting excuses, taking success and failure in stride, and paying your dues.

Resistance is a part of the human condition. You may go back through this book, and the previous one, and think of this from the point of view of a disengaged, ticked off, impaired and undereducated employee who won't do his job. It's a bit sobering. Working for you may be resistance for him. He or she may be an author.

Why People Still Don't Do Their Jobs

Links and References

# 20 Lessons from Beer

As we sign off on this journey of organizational failure, here are some lessons from beer. I know a 27-time medal winning home brewer, who is practically authoritative on beer.

There are lessons about people doing their jobs all around us, if we care to look.

Beer, in many of its forms, is a symbol of hope and progress which says that all is not yet lost.

## Lesson 1: Beer is About the Process

Here it is. There is malted barley of more than one type, which is soaked in hot water to extract the sugars. Once that is done, the sugars are boiled to crack their molecules, and hops are added to give as much hoppy flavor as you think you need.

After some amount of time, the mixture is cooled, and introduced to a sanitized container, where yeast is added. After the fermentation is done, the batch is taken off of the layer of sediment that forms, and then aged in some anaerobic environment for some length of time, usually a few days.

https://youtu.be/OyJknCLPeAk

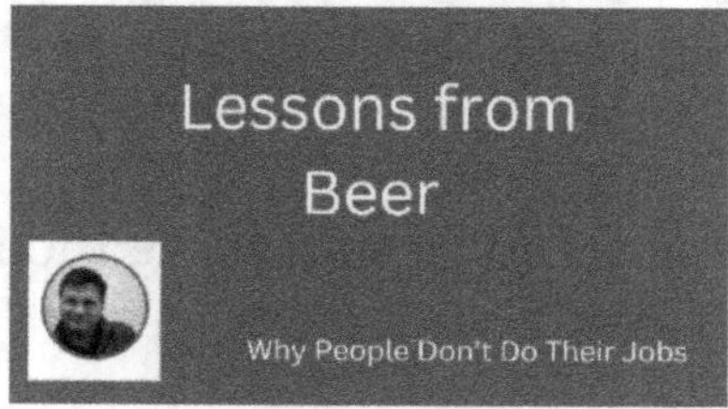

Everything in this whole process has to be sanitized, because of bacteria, which will ruin your day. There are more complications with regard to packaging.

The modern process was developed 1500 years ago by people who followed their process religiously. This was a thousand years before the invention of the microscope and discovery of bacteria.

The current accepted method for beer, which includes the addition of hops, was developed by the Benedictines, in Europe. There was an event starting in 536 AD that caused a lot of problems. This is now known as the Antique Little Ice Age, and it very nearly caused the extinction of humankind. This was in the time of St. Benedict who set up a series of monasteries throughout Europe to preserve what little civilization they could.

The Benedictine monasteries were little islands of sanity surrounded by chaos. Beer was needed to preserve as much grain as possible, and at the same time, keep the local water from making the occupants sick.

What then developed was the standard operating procedure for beer. The oldest continuously operating brewery still in existence is in Bavaria, and was established in the year 620. The brewery has outlived the monastery.

## Statistical Process Control

The father of Statistical Process Control was William Gossett, 1876-1937 better known as "Student." Gossett worked for the Guinness company, and wanted to understand the variability in his raw material supplies. He understood, and then practically applied, the practice of drawing a conclusion from some amount of data using statistical methods.

He published his work in prestigious scientific journals of the day under the name "Student" so that his competitors would not pick up on his identity.

Here is how it works: You have five samples of hops; you do a chemical analysis and the average "hops power" is measured at 5.5. You have five more samples from the next town over, and the average "hops power" is 5.7.

How do you know that the difference between 5.5 and 5.7 is "real" or not, or just some artifact of the test? The Student-t distribution, developed by this fellow, is used to make that determination. What that did was enable a set of rules for making decisions, which goes to the heart of the alarm systems and control systems we have talked about throughout this.

This was done 75 years before the invention of the graphing calculator, so these calculations must have made his head hurt.

But these same methods have been applied to everything, particularly in chemicals, and the reason we have reliable gasoline and space shuttles is this.

Everybody should know what it is, as a requirement for voting.

## Home Brewing Kits

They still sell these, although you can also get them used online at this point.

They give you a bucket, some ingredients, and some instructions. You, the prospective home brewer, have to read them and then using some equipment from your house, like your big spaghetti pot, you may attempt this process.

I would say that in this era, the era of not following directions, the chances of you getting one of these for Christmas and successfully brewing one batch of beer is probably not too good. The probability of you brewing consistent beer, year after year, of a sufficient style as to be drinkable, is nearly zero.

But if you manage to do so, don't let it sit around. Beer needs to be fresh.

Using written work instructions with no training at all is a great way to fail at anything, as we have already seen.

## Lesson 2: Beer Judging is Doing You a Favor

Here's a rule: If a beer judge tells you that your beer is not very good, that is probably true.

Not recognizing this makes you in denial, which is no way to get your beer any better.

You know those poor people who get their beer kit for the holidays, and then sometime at about the big football game they come out with their six pack of beer, and everyone tastes it and makes a face?

Well, you're not doing this fellow, and it is usually a fellow, any favors by not telling him that his beer is terrible, or that he managed to contaminate it.

There is a thing called the Beer Judge Certification Program, and there is an extensive training program and test for being a "certified beer judge." It is actually more difficult than becoming a certified ISO9001 Quality Auditor.

This is a noble cause because it is the alarm system for all of the terrible home brewers in the world. It's a way to professionally tell someone not to give up his or her day job. It also promotes literacy about the beer styles, and the historical context of some of these is very interesting.

The beer judging process is fun. Even if you are not a beer person, you can envision a big group of people, sitting around a big room somewhere, thoughtfully opening and tasting 12 entries of some weird style of beer. Well, that's what it is, and after having done it a couple of times, I can personally attest that the beer that they pick is the best in that style.

This is a worthwhile endeavor, even if only from a product quality standpoint.

If a beer judge tells you that your beer is bad, believe it, and make changes. Refusal to make changes keeps your beer bad.

## Lesson 3: Beer is Too Much Work to Make It Bad

Based on 1 and 2, above, the conclusion is that beer is too much work to make it bad. To do it right, you have to pay attention to every one of those steps I listed above, and make sure you're doing all of them under controlled conditions.

Most of the people of this era don't have the patience, nor understand control systems well enough. There is also a formulation activity as well, like recipe designing, which involves some tactile and taste ability. Ideally, there is a hard headed process person, and a more artistic taste/sight person. How they get along with your congenial sales person is the big question.

The commitment part is important. Someone that is committed to beer will do it, and fail, and admit failure, and make process modifications so that they will improve to make it judgeable.

If you're not willing to do that, then you might as well go to one of the little microbreweries that have popped up. These people are trying to live out the American Dream and provide a little beer to the world under controlled conditions, and still make money at it.

Come to think of it, they need a fourth person, an accountant, who can tell them how many people they need to get in the front door to keep it from going broke.

## Lesson 4: Beer is a Miracle of the Modern Age

Smartphones in this time period fail at the rate of 10-15%.

But when is the last time you actually had a bad commercial-scale beer? I guess it's in your definition of "bad" because some people think all of it is bad.

The modern commercial brewing process is a miracle of the modern age. You have to go through all of the above processes, keeping the whole thing sanitary, and doing it on an unimaginable scale. The storage and distribution systems have to anticipate demand fluctuations some number of weeks in advance. Everything has to be controlled, or the beer will go bad.

It has to be dropped off within a mile of your house for 99% of the population, with predictable quality.

The last tour of the day at the Miller Brewing Company main brewery in Milwaukee starts at 4 PM. I make it my business to know these things. Be prepared to walk, and climb stairs. You should take it, if you get to Milwaukee.

You may ooh and aah at the size of the operation, and try to fully appreciate all of the pumps and stainless-steel lines, and flashing lights.

What that represents is a highly developed process, and if one person in that entire complex web of events doesn't do his job, the customer doesn't get that expected experience when he or she pops the top.

I've actually been in several facilities like this, along with a high-speed full scale bottling operation, and a couple of distilleries, and have a lot of respect and appreciation for anyone who is doing this process at that scale.

You know what else is like that? Gasoline. You take a product, crude oil, which comes from the ground with all of its variability. You process it into gasoline, a highly flammable material, and then drop it off within a mile of everybody in the country with greater than 99.9% predictability. The people who are trying to do the same thing with hydrogen or electricity didn't fully appreciate the complex system we have of refineries, pipelines, blending facilities, storage, tanker truckage and delivery every 1-2 days to fill up the tanks at the local gas station. That is, unless someone doesn't do their job, and it fails.

## It's Easy to Focus on the Negative

That's about it for now.

We are surrounded by a lot of things like beer, which is made by a complex process that starts out with naturally-derived materials and reaches us in vast quantities with near perfection.

All of these things depend on people doing their jobs, and as we now know, those systems are very fragile at the moment.

Take a moment to appreciate them, when you get the chance, and while you get the chance.

Why People Still Don't Do Their Jobs

Links and References

# About the Author

Here is a little Bio information

I am a working quality auditor with more than 500 quality system audits, working with some of the global brand name companies.

My background story is in formulation development, and I am co-contributor for three US patents. After graduating from that, I used my quality systems and business analysis authority to be a contributing writer with over 1 million page views on a famous internet financial analysis website.

I also have more than 170,000 views on my YouTube site, and have been a favorite trainer and consultant on the topic of internal auditing, and the ISO9001 standard.

On my website, www.Jimshell.com, you'll find a project list, a resume and a lot of blog posts and other content that you will find entertaining and informative.

www.ingramcontent.com/pod-product-compliance
Lightning Source LLC
Chambersburg PA
CBHW071201290526
45796CB00008B/94

* 9 7 9 8 8 7 4 1 5 8 9 9 6 *